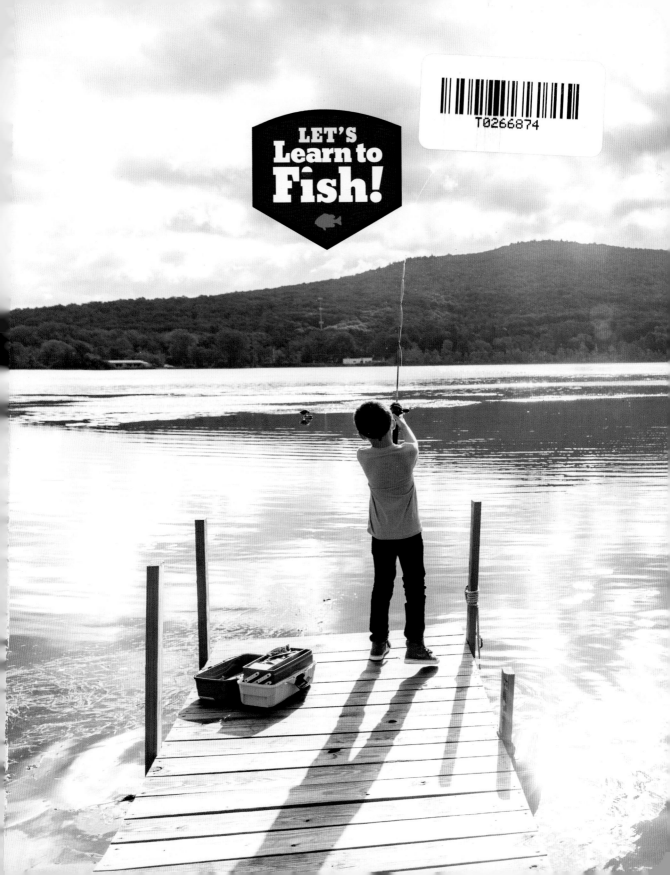

LET'S
Learn to
Fish!

LET'S Learn to Fish!

Everything You Need to Know to Start Freshwater Fishing

Dan Armitage

Storey Publishing

The mission of Storey Publishing is to serve our customers by
publishing practical information that encourages
personal independence in harmony with the environment.

Edited by Deanna F. Cook and Lisa H. Hiley

Art direction and book design by Carolyn Eckert

Text production by Liseann Karandisecky and
Jennifer Jepson Smith

Cover images by © Dan Armitage, front (b.r.); Duane Raver/
U.S. Fish and Wildlife Service/Public domain/Wikimedia
Commons, spine; © JONBOB, front (l. & m.r.), back (b.l.);
© Justin Mullet/Stocksy, back (t.); Mars Vilaubi © Storey
Publishing, front (t. & t.r.), back (b. all but l.)

Interior photography by © JONBOB

Additional photography by © Andrei Vasilev/iStock.com, 25 r.;
Andrey Trusov/Unsplash, 61; © Cara Dolan/Stocksy, 42–43;
Carolyn Eckert © Storey Publishing, 33; © Dan Armitage, 8,
92, 110 t.l., 113 t., m. & b.; Federico Giampieri/Unsplash, 116;
© GaryTalton/iStock.com, 28; Jeremy Bishop/Unsplash, 31,
99; © JP Danko/Stocksy, 110 b.r.; © Justin Mullet/Stocksy,
89; © Liam Grant/Stocksy, 100; Mars Vilaubi © Storey
Publishing, 1, 6 b.l., b.r. & t.r., 7 m.r., 12–14, 15 t., 16, 19–23, 24
t. & b., 25 all but r., 26, 27, 32, 34, 35 b.r. & m.r., 37 t.l. & t.r.,
38, 39, 40 t., 41 b.r., 47 t.l. & b.r., 57 b., 66, 70, 71, 72 l., b.c. &
b.r., 74 top all, 76, 79 b., 82, 83, 88 l., 91 b., 93 b., 110 b.l., 113
2nd fr. b., 118; © Marta Locklear/Stocksy, 40 b.; Matt Hardy/
Unsplash, 59; Matteo Bernardis/Unsplash, 3, 6 t.l.; © New
Africa/Shutterstock.com, 17 t.r.; © Nigel Cattlin/Alamy Stock
Photo, 30; Courtesy of the Recreational Boating & Fishing
Foundation, 98, 117 b.; © Ronnie Comeau/Stocksy, 97; © SDI
Productions/iStock.com, 117 t.; © Splingisv/Shutterstock.com,
60 t.; University of Washington/public domain/Wikimedia
Commons, 103 Sunfish, 104; © Willard/iStock.com, 24 m.;
© wundervisuals/iStock.com, 119

Prop styling and photo shoot assistance by Liseann Karandisecky

Illustrations by © Steve Sanford

Additional illustrations by Duane Raver/National Archives
at College Park/Still Pictures/Public domain/Wikimedia
Commons, 102 Largemouth Bass, 106; Duane Raver/
Public domain/Wikimedia Commons, 102 Catfish, 108;
Duane Raver/U.S. Fish and Wildlife Service/Public domain/
Wikimedia Commons, 102 Smallmouth Bass, 103 Crappie,
Pumpkinseed, Striped Bass & Rainbow Trout, 105, 107, 109

Text © 2024 by Dan Armitage

Storey books are available at special discounts when
purchased in bulk for premiums and sales promotions as well
as for fund-raising or educational use. Special editions or
book excerpts can also be created to specification. For details,
please send an email to special.markets@hbgusa.com.

Storey Publishing
210 MASS MoCA Way
North Adams, MA 01247
storey.com

Storey Publishing is an imprint of Workman Publishing,
a division of Hachette Book Group, Inc., 1290 Avenue of the
Americas, New York, NY 10104

Distributed in Europe by Hachette Livre,
58 rue Jean Bleuzen, 92 178 Vanves Cedex, France

Distributed in the United Kingdom by
Hachette Book Group, UK, Carmelite House,
50 Victoria Embankment, London EC4Y 0DZ

ISBNs: 978-1-63586-582-0 (paperback),
978-1-63586-583-7 (ebook)

Printed in China by R. R. Donnelley on paper from responsible
sources
10 9 8 7 6 5 4 3 2 1

Library of Congress Cataloging-in-Publication Data on file

DEDICATION

To my mom and dad,
who took me fishing,
and my son, Ethan,
who, as he grew up,
went with me.

Contents

AUTHOR'S NOTE:
The Fun of Fishing 8

1 The Basics of Tackle 11
What Is Tackle? 13
Fishing with a Handline 14
Fishing with a Cane Pole 16
Rods and Reels 18
Getting Hooked 22
Fishing Line 24
A Bit about Bobbers 24
Get Down with Sinkers 26
There's More to Tackle! 28

3 Let's Practice Rigging and Casting 43
How to Use a Cane Pole 44
How to Rig a
  Spincast Rod 50
How to Cast with a
  Spincast Rod 54

2 All about Bait 31
Types of Bait 32
Live Bait 33
Artificial Bait 38
Prepared Bait 40

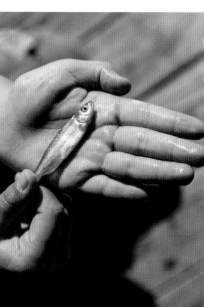

5 How to Think like a Fish 99

Comfort Zones 100

It's Fishing Season! 101

Fish You Might Catch 102

4 Time to Go Fishing! 59

Start on Shore 60

Set Up for Success 66

How to Bait a Hook 68

How to Set a Bobber 72

Cast Your Line 78

Set the Hook 80

How to Land a Fish 82

Netiquette 85

How to Remove the Hook 86

Keeping Your Catch Alive 90

How to Clean Your Catch 94

How to Cook Your Catch 96

The Tail End 110

Take Great Photos 111

An Angler's Glossary 112

Boat Safety 114

Ten Tips for Parents 117

My Fishing Logbook 120

Index 125

THE
Fun of
Fishing

Welcome to fishing!

Just by picking up this book you've taken your first step toward catching a fish. I teach fishing clinics to kids just like you around the United States, and I'm excited to share everything I know in this book. I hope that angling, which is another word for fishing, is an activity you will enjoy for years to come. One of my favorite things about fishing is that you never outgrow it. I've been fishing for more than 60 years and I'm still learning new things about how and where to catch fish. It's just as fun now as it was when I was your age!

Another thing I like about fishing is that you can keep it as simple as you want to. A cane pole with a baited hook is all you need to have fun fishing. But if you want to try different fishing tackle, which is what we call the tools for catching fish, such as rods and reels, I will show you how.

Also, fishing is an activity you can do alone or with friends and family, from shore or from a boat, and enjoy it just about anywhere you go. Fish are found everywhere!

Maybe the best thing about fishing, though, is the places you can visit to enjoy it. Lakes, streams, and other bodies of water are often located in beautiful surroundings. Even when fishing in a city, you'll have a chance to watch wildlife above and below the water's surface and to enjoy the sounds and scents of nature.

I can't wait to share my favorite sport with you, so turn the page and let's go fishing!

—**Dan Armitage**

THE BASICS OF
Tackle

You can catch fish just about any place where there is water. One of the best things about fishing is figuring out how to fool those fish into biting your bait. To do this, you'll need to round up the right equipment, or fishing tackle.

tackle box

worms

net

Your Fish Here!

spincast reel

ZEBCO 202

What Is Tackle?

Before you go fishing, you'll need to gather your tackle, or all the equipment you need to catch a fish. Fishing tackle includes things such as rods, reels, lines, hooks, bobbers, and sinkers. You can buy tackle at a bait and tackle store or at sporting goods stores.

J hook

round bobber

stick bobber

rod & reel

6 lb fishing line

sinkers

Fishing with a Handline

Most anglers tie their line to the end of a fishing pole or rod made of bamboo cane, wood, aluminum, graphite, or fiberglass, and we'll talk more about that. The simplest fishing tackle, though, is a piece of string or line with a fishing hook tied to the end. Really, this could be all you need to catch a fish!

People all over the world use nothing more than a line and a baited hook to catch fish, a practice called handlining. Shown here is a readily available type of handlining tool called a Cuban yo-yo. It makes things easier to have a handle to hold and to wind the line onto.

The great thing about handlines is that they're lightweight and small. You can carry one in your backpack so you can fish anywhere you find yourself (so long as you can find bait). They're convenient for fishing off a dock or from a boat—just unwind the baited line, cast it (as shown below), and wait for a fish! You may also want to tie a weight to the line, since handlines cast better with a weight attached.

When casting with a handline, make sure you hold the handle, not the line. Fish swim fast and pull the line quickly, which might cut your hand.

Cuban yo-yo

How to Cast with a Cuban Yo-Yo

Wide edge

Hold the yo-yo in one hand with the narrow edge facing your palm. The wide edge is curved to let the line spool off it easily. With your other hand, hold the line about a foot above the baited hook and pull off a couple of feet of line.

Spin up and away

Point the center of the yo-yo in the direction you want to cast your line. Spin the hook a few times and let it go over the water as though throwing an underhand ball.

Wind the yo-yo, not the line

To reel in the line, move the yo-yo in circles around the line rather than trying to wind the line itself. This gives you more control over the line when you are bringing in a fish.

BOTTLE HANDLINING

Turn a plastic bottle into a simple handline and cast away!

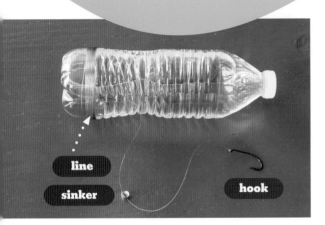

line

sinker

hook

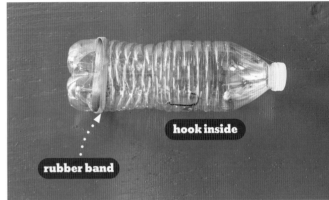

hook inside

rubber band

You can make an inexpensive handline with a plastic bottle and cap, a hook, and a sinker. Tie one end of the line around the bottom of the bottle and wrap about 20 feet of line around the bottle. Tie the hook to the other end of the line. Add a sinker to provide weight so you can cast the line far enough into the water.

To store your handline, wrap the line around the bottle to keep it from tangling. Put a rubber band around your line so it stays in place and doesn't unravel. Insert the hook in the bottle and screw the cap on to store the hook safely.

TIP: You can also use the bottle to store minnows and other live bait for under an hour. Fill the bottle with water from the lake and put your extra minnows in the bottle. Gently shake the bottle occasionally to aerate the water for the minnows.

Don't let go of the bottle!

worm

Unwind some line and toss the bait as far as you can, using your arm like a fishing rod.

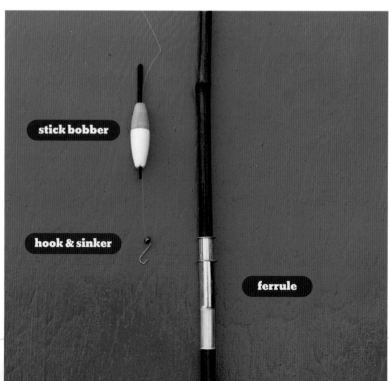

Fishing with a Cane Pole

I recommend that beginning anglers of any age use a cane pole when learning the basics of fishing. Rigged with a line, a hook, and a bobber, this is the easiest tackle to use.

You just bait the hook with a worm—there are no reels to mess with. Drop the baited line and bobber into water along the shore. (Learn how to bait a hook on page 68, and more about bobbers on page 24.) When the bobber starts to bob, or jiggle, or is suddenly pulled underwater by a fish that has grabbed the bait, the fun of catching a fish begins. You never know what kind of fish it might be or how big or small it is until you see it swimming and splashing on the surface! (Learn how to use a cane pole on page 44.)

The thing about cane poles is that the line is only as long as the pole is, so you can only send your bait out about that far. That usually isn't a problem when you're fishing near shore or from a dock, because many fish like to swim around the rocks, weeds, fallen trees, and brush that are often found close to shore.

Make sure the hook is in this position when you're not using the pole so it doesn't catch on anything.

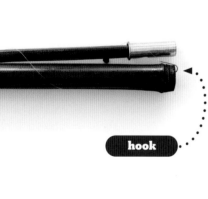

hook

stick bobber

hook & sinker

ferrule

When you hook a fish, lift up the tip of the rod or back up to bring your catch out of the water and on to shore.

CUT YOUR OWN CANE POLE

People around the world have been using bamboo canes as fishing poles for thousands of years. Bamboo is a type of grass, and it is one of the fastest-growing plants in the world. Bamboo cane can grow to 50 feet high or more. It is a popular ornamental plant, so you might even spy a grove of bamboo in your own neighborhood.

To use bamboo or any other kind of cane as a fishing rod, cut down a stalk, strip off the branches and leaves, and cut the cane to the correct length for you. Ten feet is a good length to start with. Let it dry in the sun for a few days or weeks. Then simply tie your fishing line to the tip and go fish!

Rods and Reels

A rod and reel combo is the next step up from a cane pole. The reel, where a lot of line can be stored, allows you to cast the baited line farther over the water to where fish might be hanging out. After casting, you wind the line back in to see if a fish will strike the bait. If not, you cast again!

Fishing rods are narrow and flexible and can be anywhere from 3 feet to more than 20 feet long. Most rods measure 5 to 7 feet long. The flexibility makes it easier to cast the bait farther out across the water. It also makes it easier to bring a fish in to the shore or boat. The fish gets tired tugging on the bending tip of the rod, and the way the rod gives makes it harder for a larger fish to break the line.

drag An adjustable brake that releases the line under tension if a big fish is pulling on it

line release button Holds the line on the spool when pushed down and releases the line for casting when it's let go

reel cover Protects the spool, where the wound-up line is stored

handle For rewinding the line onto the spool

Spincast Reel

The most common fishing reel and the easiest to learn how to use is the spincast reel. It has two features that make it especially simple to use: a spool that holds the fishing line and a push button that stops or releases the line.

The reel "seat" is the spot on the rod where the reel attaches. A spincast reel sits on a seat on top of the rod, with the spool facing forward toward the rod's tip. The line running from the spool to the tip is held in place by a series of little metal hoops, called line guides, along the top of the rod.

The way the line comes easily off the spool makes the spincast reel easy to cast, while the push-button brake allows you to control the line during the cast. A handle on the side of the reel is used to crank in the line and bait (or a fish, if you're lucky!).

Casting is when you toss your baited hook or lure out into the water to see if a fish will bite it.

drag

An adjustable brake that releases the line under tension if a big fish is pulling on it

bail

spool

For storing the line

line roller

handle

For rewinding the line onto the spool

Spinning and Casting Reels

There are two other popular types of fishing reels: spinning reels and casting reels.

A spinning reel must be matched with a spinning rod, which has its reel seat and line guides on its underside. A spinning reel also has a wire hoop, called a bail, to catch the line and wrap it around the spool automatically as the angler turns the reel handle.

It takes a bit more practice to learn how to cast with a spinning reel because instead of a push button to automatically hold the line or release it from the spool, the angler has to use the index finger on their casting hand. They hold the line with their finger to keep it from unwinding off the spool until the cast is made, then release the line at the just right moment to allow it to be pulled off the spool by the weight of the bait or lure.

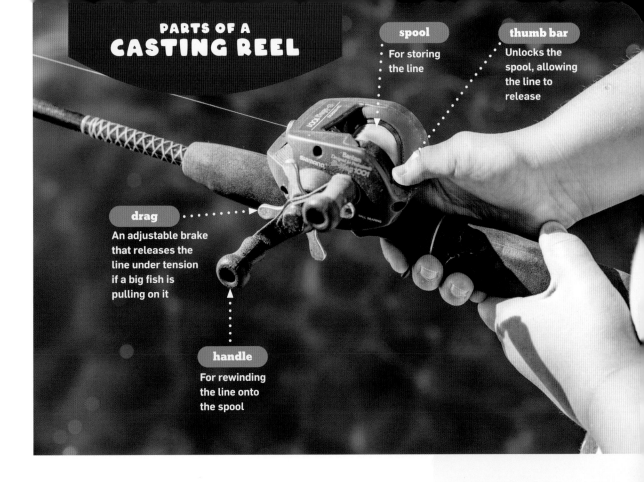

PARTS OF A
CASTING REEL

spool
For storing the line

thumb bar
Unlocks the spool, allowing the line to release

drag
An adjustable brake that releases the line under tension if a big fish is pulling on it

handle
For rewinding the line onto the spool

A casting reel (also called a baitcasting reel or level-wind reel) attaches to a reel seat on the top side of the rod's handle, like a spincast reel. The spool doesn't face forward toward the rod tip but sits sideways in the reel, where you can see the spool rotating as it releases or brings in line through guides on the top side of the rod.

Some casting reels have a push button to release and stop the line, like spincast reels, while others (shown above) require anglers to use their thumb to slow or stop the line, like spinning reels. That is why many anglers feel that casting reels are the most accurate when, well, casting! It takes some practice to learn to release the line at the right time.

FISHING POLE OR FISHING ROD?

Do you know the difference between a fishing pole and a fishing rod?

A fishing **pole** is made of natural material, such as bamboo cane, willow, or hickory. A fishing **rod** is made from fiberglass, graphite, aluminum, or steel. Most rods matched with a reel are made of fiberglass, graphite, or a combination of these manufactured materials.

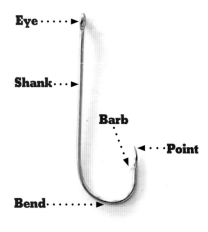

Eye · · · · · ▶

Shank · · · ▶

Barb

◀ · · · Point

Bend · · · · · · · · ▶

Getting Hooked

Fishing hooks are stamped out of bronze or made of thin metal wire bent into a J shape. They are sharpened at one end and have a small loop or "eye" at the other for tying the hook to a line. Hooks come in all sizes, from tiny ones for catching small fish with small mouths to giant hooks for catching big fish with big mouths.

Most fishing hooks also have a barb, a small, rear-facing point just behind the big point of the hook. The barb has two jobs: to help keep bait on the hook and to help keep the hook stuck in a fish's mouth once it bites the bait. Some catch-and-release anglers (who put their fish back into the water after they catch them) use barbless hooks to make it easier to remove the hook from the fish's mouth.

If you're using minnows and worms for bait, a good hook to start with is a size 8. This size is large enough to hold the bait and small enough to allow the bait to move around naturally. Also, a size 8 fits inside the smaller mouths of sunfish but is big enough to hook larger fish, such as bass or catfish, that might come along!

Go for the Gold

Most fishing hooks are made of bronze, a dark brown metal. Hooks made of wire are gold colored. I recommend wire hooks when you're using minnows for bait because they are thinner and easier to stick into the mouth or skin of the minnow. Wire hooks also weigh less, so the baitfish can swim around more easily and look more natural to the fish you are trying to fool into grabbing them. And wire hooks are easier to stick into worms, too.

FIRST HOOKS

The first fishing hooks, used thousands of years ago, were made of bone, shell, antler, or wood. Instead of being curved, some were sharpened on both ends, sort of like a fat toothpick. The line was tied to the middle of the stick and the hook was stuck into the bait. When a fish ate the bait, the angler pulled on the line and hoped the sharp ends would catch in the fish's mouth as it was pulled in.

BIGGER IS SMALLER

Bigger hooks have smaller numbers.
Smaller hooks have bigger numbers.

It may seem backward, but the smaller the hook, the higher the number that is used to identify it! So, a size 12 hook is smaller than a size 6 hook and much smaller than a size 1 hook.

If that isn't confusing enough, hooks larger than a size 1 are the opposite: A 1/0 hook (pronounced "one ought") is smaller than a size 2/0 hook and much smaller than the largest hook made for recreational fishing, a size 12/0.

When in doubt, use a smaller hook, at least to start. As the saying goes:

You can catch a big fish with a small hook, but not a small fish with a big hook!

#2
#4
#6
#8
#10
#12

A size 8 hook is a good size to start with.
It works with many types of bait and can catch fish of different sizes.

types of hooks

J hook
A wire J hook is a good general-purpose hook for most fishing expeditions.

Baitholder hook
To help keep live bait on it, this hook has a barb on the shank as well as one on the curved part.

Circle hook
This hook can be used with live and prepared baits. It is designed to hook the fish's lips rather than being swallowed.

Treble hook
A treble hook is used for dough and prepared baits and on artificial lures.

Fishing Line

Clear monofilament nylon line that tests between 6 and 10 pounds is a good choice for most situations.

There are many kinds of line made just for fishing. Anglers try to use the thinnest line possible to pull in the kind of fish they hope to catch. Thinner line is easier to cast out over the water and harder for the fish to see. But the thinner the line is, the more easily it can break when a big fish pulls on it.

The best line to use is clear monofilament nylon line that "tests" between 6 and 10 pounds before breaking. That's thin enough not to scare fish but strong enough to pull in a nice-sized catch!

A Bit about Bobbers

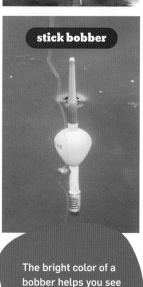

round bobber

stick bobber

The bright color of a bobber helps you see it in the water.

Bobbers, also called floats, are small, buoyant objects that anglers attach to their fishing line to do three things:

- Keep the bait suspended at a certain depth
- Show the angler where the bait is located
- Alert the angler when a fish is chasing or eating the bait

Bobbers are made of hollow plastic, wood, foam, or cork. They range in size—some are smaller than a fingernail while others are as big as a baseball. They come in a variety of shapes as well, depending on how they are going to be used for fishing and the size and weight of the bait they are expected to suspend.

Bobbers are usually used when you are fishing with live bait.

Round bobbers, a common choice, are about an inch in diameter and made of hollow plastic. Most are red and white or other bright colors so you can see them on top of the water.

Stick bobbers are used when you are fishing for species that may spit out your bait if they feel any resistance from the float. Because they are so narrow, these bobbers are easy for fish to pull under when they swim off with the bait.

HOMEMADE BOBBER

Make your own bobber from a cork!

Cut through the side of the cork, slicing halfway through it.

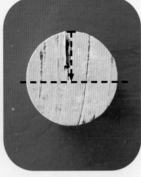

A cork that is 1 to 2 inches long and three-quarters of an inch in diameter is just the right size. You can reuse a cork from a bottle or find one at a craft store. To make a bobber, carefully cut a slit down the length of the cork with a sharp knife. Cut about halfway through the cork.

Slide the fishing line into the slice you made in the cork.

Slide the fishing line into the slit, where it will stay in place. Now you have a bobber! When you hook a fish, the cork should stay on the line, but carry a few spare corks in case one falls off while you are casting or landing a fish. Between casts, check to make sure the cork is securely on the line.

Cork comes from the inner bark of the cork oak tree. It's perfect for making bobbers because it floats and doesn't absorb water—and, because it's natural, it's okay for the environment if you lose one!

SUPER-SKINNY STICK BOBBERS

Some bobbers are made from porcupine quills. These super-skinny bobbers are used by anglers who fish for very wary fish species, such as crappies and trout.

When a fish takes the bait, a quill bobber is so long and narrow that it will slip under the water with very little resistance. That means the fish is less likely to feel the bobber and spit out the bait before you can set the hook and reel in the fish. Modern stick bobbers work much the same way.

Get Down with Sinkers

Sinkers are small weights, made of soft metal such as lead or tungsten, that are put on the fishing line. The extra weight helps the bait sink and makes it easier to cast the line when you're using a fishing reel.

Split shot are small round sinkers, with a slot where the line goes. To attach a split shot to your line, slide the line into the slot, then use pliers to pinch the sinker on tightly. You can use more than one split shot on the line to get the weight you need.

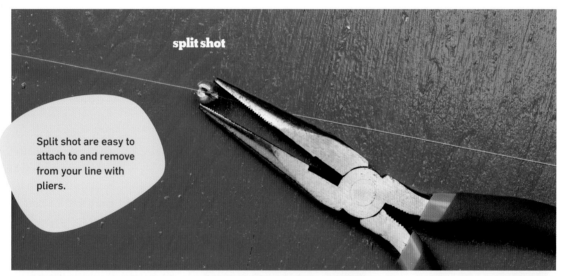

split shot

Split shot are easy to attach to and remove from your line with pliers.

To attach a split shot to the line, use pliers to pinch the "mouth" tightly.

To remove the split shot, position the pliers on the open "butterfly wings."

Pinch the butterfly wings tightly and the mouth will open to release the line.

Bank or dipsey sinkers are larger than split shot and designed to keep the bait down at the bottom. The line is threaded through a loop at the top of the sinker. When a fish takes the bait and swims away, the line slides through the loop so the fish doesn't feel any resistance and spit out the bait.

Egg sinkers are round or oval and have a hole through them, from end to end, to allow the line to slide through so a fish doesn't feel the sinker's weight.

The hooks, sinkers, snaps, and bobbers that you tie onto the end of your fishing line are called terminal tackle because they are placed on the "terminal" or end of the line. You don't always use all of them, but it's good to have a selection of each when you go fishing in case you need them.

egg sinker

dipsey sinker

split shot
Split shot comes in various sizes.

1 foot

snap swivel

Some anglers tie a snap swivel to the end of their line. It makes it quick and easy to change hooks or lures and keeps the line from getting twisted as you reel it in.

There's More to Tackle!

While it's true that you don't need more than a pole, a hook, and some bait to catch fish, having a few other pieces of equipment will make your fishing adventure safer and more efficient. For starters, it makes sense to have extra hooks, bobbers, and sinkers in case you need to change sizes or you lose tackle to a snag or a big fish.

A tackle box makes it easy to carry and store your gear. Some tackle boxes have compartments or trays to organize and protect your supplies. Most are made of plastic or aluminum and have lids that snap shut. You can also use a shoebox or plastic container, a heavy plastic bag, or a backpack or tote bag to carry your fishing tackle.

Needle-nose pliers have long, pointy jaws that can be used to remove a hook from a fish's mouth (or other places where fishing hooks can get stuck), to pinch a sinker onto the line, and to pull a knot tight. Pick needle-nose pliers that include cutting blades and you can also use them to cut fishing line. You can buy them at any hardware store, and most bait and tackle shops offer specialized fishing pliers.

A landing net lets you scoop a wriggling fish out of the water and transfer it to land. A fish weighs lots more out of the water than in it. If you lift a fish out of the water with just your fishing line, the line may break or the hook could pull free, letting the fish get away. You may not need a net for smaller panfish such as sunfish or crappies, but it doesn't hurt to use one just in case.

You may want a short net for use in a shallow stream or a low-profile boat and a long one for reaching from a dock or a larger boat. A landing net with a hoop that is about a foot and a half in diameter with a handle one to two feet long is a good all-around choice for most freshwater fishing situations.

A cotton hand towel or washcloth comes in handy for cleaning your hands after handling worms or minnows. If you're going to keep a fish you've caught, a towel can also help you hold on to it when removing the hook. I put a towel on a metal shower-curtain hook, which I attach to my belt or the handle of my tackle box to keep it handy.

FRY 'EM UP!

Sunfish and crappies, as well as rock bass and white bass, are often called panfish because they are the perfect size to fit in a frying pan!

Find out how to set up your fishing spot for success on page 66.

tackle box

minnow bucket

bait box

landing nets

rod and reel

needle-nose pliers

Extras. A portable chair is nice to have so that you can sit down and get comfortable between bites. A hat with a brim or bill is good for shading your head and eyes from the sun, as are sunglasses. A cooler with snacks and drinks will keep your energy up for a full day of fun. And don't forget a camera or cell phone so you can take photos and share your fishing adventure with family and friends.

SUNGLASSES SAVE THE DAY

Sunglasses do three things for anglers who wear them: They protect your eyes from the bright rays of the sun, they cut the glare from the water's surface so you can see what's below, and they protect your eyes from accidentally getting poked by a fishing rod or hook. So even if the sun is not shining brightly, it's a good idea to wear sunglasses while fishing.

And it's always a good idea to know where your rod tip is pointed and who is around you when you cast so that you don't accidentally poke or hook yourself or others.

ALL ABOUT Bait

One of the best things about fishing is figuring out how to get the fish to bite your baited hook. You'll learn how to put bait on a hook in Chapter 4, but first let's talk about the different types of bait we use to attract different kinds of fish.

Types of Bait

Bait is anything placed on a hook or tied to the end of the line to fool a fish into taking the hook into its mouth. There are three main categories: live, artificial, and prepared.

Live bait is a creature that fish like to eat, such as a worm. You put it on the hook while it is alive, and its scent and movement in the water attract fish.

Artificial bait looks like something a fish would eat but it's made of rubber, plastic, or some other material. An artificial bait, or lure, often has a hook already attached.

You usually have to make the lure move in the water to get the attention of the fish, although some artificial soft plastic baits are infused with scent.

Prepared bait looks like colorful clay but tastes and smells like fish food. You put a lump of it on your hook, and as it melts in the water, the sight and scent bring fish around to consider eating it. You can also use bread, hot dogs, and soft cheese as bait. Yep, fish like to eat some of the same foods you do!

live bait

artificial bait

live bait

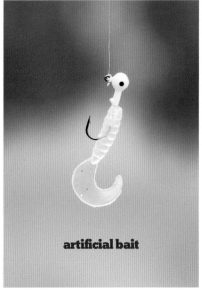

artificial bait

prepared bait

Live Bait

Live bait is the best choice for beginners. It catches many types of fish and is easy to use. You can buy worms, minnows, and other live bait at any bait and tackle store and at many larger retail stores that sell fishing tackle. But many anglers like to find their own live bait. It can be almost as much fun as catching a fish!

Worms Rule

By far the most popular live bait to use for freshwater fishing is an earthworm, the kind you find in your garden or on the sidewalk after it rains. Other kinds of worms are also used for bait, including small red worms an inch or two long and large nightcrawlers that may be a foot in length! Most fish love to eat any kind of worm they swim across. Fish naturally find earthworms that are washed into the water by rains or floods.

The smaller fish species beginners fish for love to eat worms and don't grow very big, so start out using regular earthworms. They are easy to put on a small hook and stay lively and wiggling when placed in the water. If you have nightcrawlers, you can cut them into pieces to make them more the size of earthworms.

Buying Worms

Worms usually come in a plastic carton, like the kind cottage cheese comes in. Inside the carton is bedding, which might be soil, moss, or even shredded newspaper, for the worms to burrow under. The worms can live in that carton for several weeks if you keep it in a cool place, like the corner of your basement or in the refrigerator, and give them some food. You can buy worm food at the bait store, or just sprinkle some cornmeal or white flour on top of the bedding.

Be sure to ask permission before putting worms in the fridge. Some adults may not want a surprise when they open a carton that they think has people food inside!

SUPPORT YOUR LOCAL BAIT STORE

Talking to the folks at your local bait store is a great way to gather local fishing information. You can support your local bait and tackle store by purchasing more than just bait there. Most bait stores don't make much money by selling worms, minnows, and other bait. Providing live bait to anglers is just a way to get customers to come to the store, where they will also hopefully buy the tackle they need.

That is how bait and tackle shops make enough money to stay in business. If we don't support them by buying our tackle from them, they will go away. Then where will we go to buy live bait and get the latest local fishing advice?

COLLECTING WORMS

Earthworms live underground, tunneling through the soil as they eat dirt and plant debris. There are several subspecies of earthworms, including small red worms and large nightcrawlers. They all work great as bait.

DIG 'EM UP

A good place to look for worms is a flower or vegetable garden.

Grab a shovel or trowel and a container with a lid. Put some dirt or worm bedding in the container. Then dig up a clump of soil and crumble it to expose the worms for easy picking. Handling the worms gently, place them on top of the soil or bedding in your bait container.

Healthy worms will dig into the bedding right away. Any worms that don't disappear into the soil after an hour or so may be injured and should be placed back in the garden.

RAIN, RAIN, COME MY WAY

When the ground is soaked, worms come to the surface. Go outside after a heavy rain and pick up worms you find on pavement. You can often gather dozens of worms in a short time.

LET THERE BE LIGHT

Head out onto your lawn after dark with your worm container and a flashlight or a headlamp. Some worm pickers use a red lens on their lamp because worms seem less likely to disappear back into the ground when they are struck by red light rather than white light.

You can water the lawn first to help get the worms to move to the surface. Walk slowly and softly so that the vibrations of your footsteps don't scare the worms, and start searching for the shine of a worm in the grass.

As soon as you spot a worm, quickly grab it before it pulls itself back into its hole. Nightcrawlers especially will keep one end in their hole and will break in half if you try to pull them out. Instead, hold firmly and wait. The worm will eventually release its grip on the dirt, and then you can pull it out and drop it into your bait container.

Minnows Make Great Bait

Minnows may look like baby fish, but they are just a type of fish that doesn't grow very large. They are also called "baitfish" because they are often used as bait to catch bigger fish. There are many species of minnows, and they are different in different parts of the country. Your local bait store will sell the type of minnow that is best to use as bait for your area, as well as traps if you want to catch them yourself.

Minnow maintenance. Minnows are a little harder to keep alive than worms. It's easy enough to put them in a bucket of water, but after a while they will use up all the oxygen in the water and won't be able to breathe. If you buy them right before a fishing trip, you can put them in a special bait bucket with holes in it that you place in the pond or stream where you are fishing. The holes allow water to pass through so there is always enough oxygen for the minnows.

To keep them alive longer, like overnight, you can use a plug-in or battery-powered aerator with a hose to pump oxygen into the bucket of water.

Water safety. Try not to use water straight from the faucet for keeping minnows. Most tap water has chemicals in it to make it safe to drink, but those chemicals can harm minnows. Instead, use bottled water, rainwater, or water from a lake or stream. If you must use tap water, fill the bucket and let it sit uncovered overnight. That will allow some of the chemicals to evaporate before you place any minnows into the water.

You may be able to catch your own minnows to use as bait by tossing out a simple fish trap a few hours before you plan to go fishing.

minnow

aerator

Try Grubs!

Another excellent bait, especially for panfish, is grubs, which are the larvae (young form) of different kinds of insects. The larvae eventually will grow into whatever type of insect laid the eggs, but when they are in grub stage, they look like short worms and fish love to eat them. You can buy grubs at the bait store in covered plastic cups with sawdust as bedding.

The most popular grubs for bait are mealworms, which are about half an inch long and have a light brown skin that feels hard to the touch. Waxworms, another popular bait, are smaller and softer-skinned than mealworms. I recommend using mealworms because they are easier to handle and put on the hook.

Mealworms are easy to keep between fishing trips for as long as a month if they are kept cool. They don't need to be fed.

MAKE A CRICKET TRAP

Catch your own bait in the backyard with a loaf of bread.

1. Like worms, crickets make good bait and are easily caught. They're active at night and will eat almost anything. Cut an unsliced loaf of bread in half as shown. Cut small holes in each end and hollow out the loaf.

2. Use large rubber bands to hold the two halves together. Crickets will enter through the holes and stay inside to eat. In the evening, set the loaf out in a field or other area with long grass (not a mowed lawn).

3. Early in the morning, carefully open your bread trap to see what's there. Grab the crickets and put them in a cricket cage (shown above). Or you can put them in a plastic tub with holes punched in the lid.

4. You can hook a cricket just about anywhere on its body, but behind the head is an especially good location.

Artificial Bait

Artificial baits, sometimes called lures, are made to look like all kinds of things that fish like to eat. Most of them have a hook or hooks attached. Many recreational anglers like lures because of the added challenge of fooling the fish into biting. Using a lure requires more activity from the angler, who has to make the lure move like something alive.

artificial worm

Artificial worms are made from flexible rubber or plastic. Because the material feels soft, like a real worm, a fish won't spit it out right away, giving the angler extra time to pull up on the line and hook the fish.

Artificial minnows come in hundreds of shapes, sizes, and colors to try to match what the minnows look like in the waters where they will be used to catch fish. Minnow lures also come in models that float, sink, or dive under the water when you reel in the line.

When you're out fishing, you can experiment with different kinds of artificial minnow lures to find out where the fish are feeding on real minnows, anywhere from the water's surface to the bottom, and then use an artificial minnow that goes to that depth when you are reeling it back in.

artificial minnow

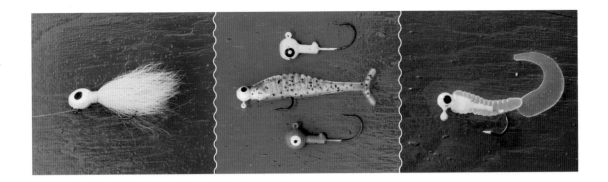

Jigs

A jig is a hook with weight attached to it. Plain jigs are meant to be used with bait, such as a minnow or worm. Some jigs are "dressed" with feathers, hair, or plastic tails that make them look like something a fish would want to eat. Jigs are made of soft, heavy metal that can be molded around the eye end of the hook. They may be left natural or painted in bright colors.

A jig is balanced so that the pointed end of the hook rides up, which helps keep it from getting caught on rocks or weeds. That is important, because jigs sink quickly and are usually used to catch fish that are feeding close to the bottom. To use a jig, you cast it into the water, let it sink to the bottom or to a depth where you think fish might be hanging out, and start reeling it in. It often helps to twitch the tip of the rod to give the jig more action, which may make a fish decide to try to eat it.

Some jigs have feathers or fur to make them look more natural to the fish.

WHAT'S THE ANGLE?

Another word for fishing is *angling*. Someone who fishes is an angler. Why? Well, many centuries ago, fishing hooks were called angles because they were bent to hold bait and hook fish.

Nowadays an angler is someone who fishes for pleasure rather than a professional who catches fish to sell. And small worms, one of the most popular live baits, are often called angleworms.

cheese

bread

Dampen and squeeze bread into a ball so it stays on the hook longer.

hot dog

Prepared Bait

You can buy prepared bait that is made of a mixture of things fish like to eat. It comes in a jar or a tub and looks and feels like colorful cookie dough. When this type of bait hits the water, it slowly melts and sends flavor into the water around it for the fish to smell and be attracted by.

Prepared bait is handy because it doesn't require any special care, like keeping it cool, and if you keep the container tightly covered, it lasts a long time. There are many types and flavors of prepared baits, most of which work for the panfish we want to catch. Ask someone working at the bait and tackle shop what kind or flavor of prepared bait they recommend for the place where you plan to go fishing.

Kitchen scraps. You might find a version of prepared bait right in your kitchen. Fish like to eat some of the same things that we do. Bread, hot dogs, corn, and cheese are popular with a variety of fish.

You can use bait from home any time you don't have live bait. Many anglers actually prefer to use homemade bait to catch a particular fish species. Trout love to eat kernels of canned corn or cheese balls, for example. Catfish and most panfish will attack bread balls and pieces of hot dog or bologna placed on a hook.

ODD BAITS

Anglers use all kinds of things for fishing bait. A bar of hand soap cut into cubes is popular with some people who fish for catfish. Carp anglers make their own dough from bread or breakfast cereal softened with water and flavored with all kinds of things, including gelatin powder, honey, anise oil, strawberry soda pop, and even goose poop!

HOW TO USE PREPARED BAIT

A jar of bait is easy to use and convenient to store.

 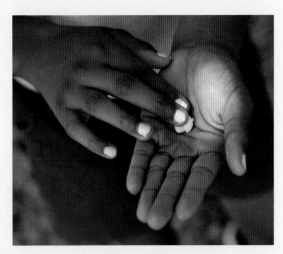

1. Roll a small piece into a ball about the size of the curved part of your hook.

2. Push the point of the hook into the bait ball until the bend and point are covered.

LET'S PRACTICE Rigging and Casting

I know you're excited to start fishing, but I always recommend that beginners practice with their equipment before trying to catch a fish. Get comfortable rigging your rod with a bobber, sinker, and baited hook. Spend some time practicing casting to get your bait to land where you want it to. A little bit of practice means you'll have more fun when you're out on a fishing adventure.

We'll start by practicing with a cane pole, which doesn't require a reel, and then move on to a rod-and-reel rig.

HOW TO Use a Cane Pole

Most anglers buy their cane poles as packaged kits that include a hook, sinker, bobber, and line. The poles are usually 10 feet long and come in two pieces to make them easier to carry around. Here's how to set up a cane pole if it isn't already rigged.

WHAT YOU NEED

- Cane pole
- Fishing line with hook
- Sinker
- Bobber

10 feet!

RIG THE POLE

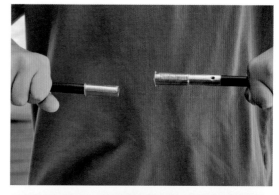

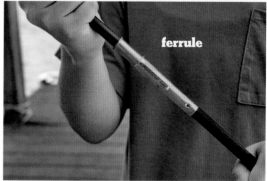

ferrule

1   Put the two parts of the pole together with the metal connector, called a ferrule.

2 Unwrap a few feet of the fishing line. In most kits, the hook and sometimes a bobber are already attached to the line.

3 Carefully tuck the bend of the hook into the hollow butt end of the pole.

hook

butt end ▼

line

tip of rod

4 Gently pulling on the line to keep the hook attached to the pole, measure out a length of line that is as long as the pole.

How to Use a Cane Pole continued

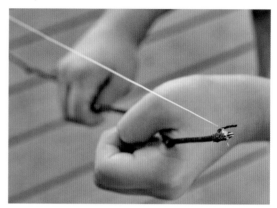

5   Cut the line and tie it to the small metal eye at the end of the pole using an improved clinch knot
    (see illustration). If the pole doesn't have an eye, tie the line securely to the end of the cane.
    With the knot, the line will be slightly shorter than the cane pole, and the tension on the line will
    bend the end of the pole a little bit to help hold the hook in the butt end.

HOW TO TIE AN IMPROVED CLINCH KNOT

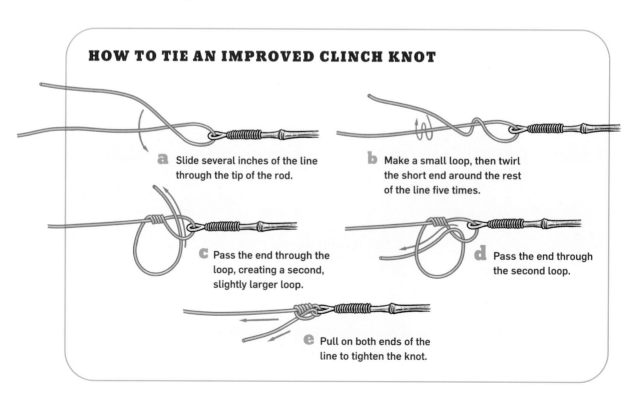

a   Slide several inches of the line
    through the tip of the rod.

b   Make a small loop, then twirl
    the short end around the rest
    of the line five times.

c   Pass the end through the
    loop, creating a second,
    slightly larger loop.

d   Pass the end through
    the second loop.

e   Pull on both ends of the
    line to tighten the knot.

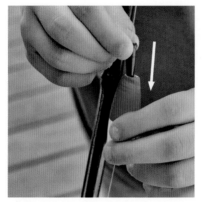

bobber with stopper peg

6 Set the bobber on the line 2 to 3 feet up from the hook. This type of bobber has a stopper peg that holds it on the line. Slip the bobber on the line and push the peg in to wedge it in place. To move the bobber along the line, pull out and replace the peg. (See Chapter 4 for more details on setting a bobber.)

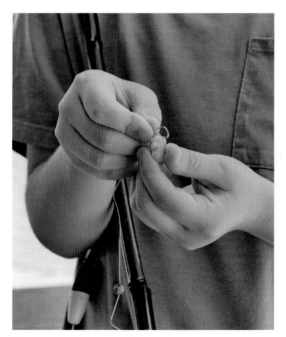

7 Bait the hook with a ball of cheese or piece of hot dog.

PRACTICE WITH A CASTING PLUG

You can buy a weighted casting plug made of rubber, with no hook, that is designed to allow you to practice casting without the tangles—and potential punctures!—that would result if you used a real hook, weight, and bobber.

You can also use a quarter-ounce dipsey or bank sinker.

How to Use a Cane Pole continued

bobber

hook and worm

CASTING

1 Hold the thick butt end of the cane pole in one or both hands. Point the tip almost straight up in front of you or to one side, high enough that the hook is off the ground or out of the water.

bobber

hook and worm

2 Carefully swing the pole to carry the line and hook out over the area where you want the bait to land. Keep practicing until you get the feel of how fast to swing the pole. Watch out for the hook as it flies through the air!

STORING A CANE POLE

Putting your equipment away properly is an important part of being a good angler. Don't leave it lying around where someone might step on it and break your pole or, worse, get a hook in their foot.

To store your cane pole between uses, carefully pull the hook down toward the butt end of the pole, which will bend the pole slightly, and tuck the point of the hook into the butt end. The tension of the bent pole will keep the hook in place.

For longer-term storage, take the pole apart and wrap the line around the two pieces to keep them together. You can remove the hook and bobber from the line or leave them attached. Wrap the line all the way to its end and tuck the point of the hook into the butt end of the pole to keep it secure.

Rig a Spincast Rod

Every beginning angler should practice casting with a spincast rod before taking it to the water to fish. Here, we'll go through the steps of rigging a spincast rod for practice casting, with a sinker or practice plug at the end of the line instead of a hook.

Once you have the hang of it, replace the sinker or practice plug with a baited hook or fishing lure, and you'll be ready to catch some fish!

WHAT YOU NEED

- **Rod and reel rig**
- **Fishing line**
- **Sinker**

1 If the reel is not already secured to the rod, clip it into place. The reel has a foot that fits into a slot on the reel seat.

2 Secure the reel by screwing down the threaded ring that locks it in place.

threaded ring

3 Push and release the button on the back of the reel to release the line inside the reel. You may have to unscrew the reel's face cover to locate the end of the line.

face cover

4 Make a small loop at the end of the line and thread it through the hole in the reel's face cover. Then screw the face cover back in place.

line guide

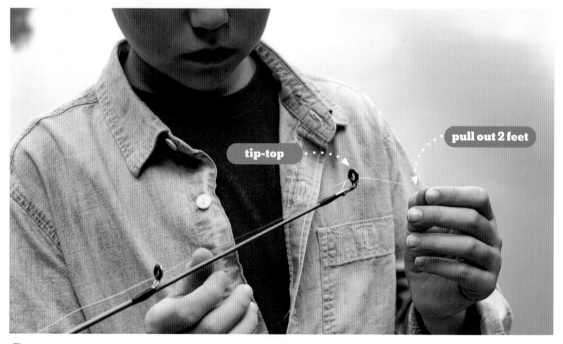

tip-top

pull out 2 feet

5 Thread the line through all the guides along the rod and out the last one, called the tip-top. Keep pulling out line until you have about 2 feet of free line at the end of the rod.

6 Tie the end of the line to a sinker or practice plug using an improved clinch knot. Crank the reel handle to rewind the line until the sinker is pulled tight against the tip-top so it won't get tangled around the tip of the rod.

HOW TO TIE ON A HOOK

The same knot is used to tie on a hook as to tie the line to the rod. See the steps on page 46.

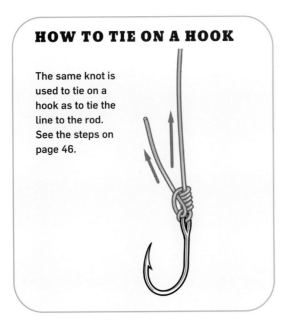

To practice casting, tie a sinker on your line in the same way.

HOW TO Cast with a Spincast Rod

Find an open lawn or parking area where there aren't any trees or bushes to tangle your line. Set out a target, like a plastic hoop or trash can lid, and make a game out of seeing how far and how accurately you can cast the sinker.

1 Hold the rod in one hand, with the reel on top of the rod. Most spincast rods have a trigger-shaped extension on the underside of the reel seat that you can wrap your index finger around to give you a better grip.

2 Push the line-release button with your thumb. Release the button to let the line run out about a foot, so that the sinker dangles from the end of the rod, and then push and hold the button down to keep more line from coming out of the reel.

1 foot

sinker · · · ▸

3 Face your target. Keeping the button pushed down to hold the line, slowly bring the tip of the rod back behind your head, until the rod points at an angle behind you.

Try to keep your elbow close to your side when you swing the rod behind you to cast, and make sure the sinker is not tangled around the rod tip before you start to swing the rod forward.

↓

4 Keep your eye on the target and your thumb holding the line release button down. When you are ready to cast, quickly whip the tip of the rod forward (4a) to point at your target, while at the same time taking your thumb off the button to release the line (4b).

It may take a few tries, but you'll quickly learn the right timing for when to take your thumb off the button.

↓

The casting action all together!

Take your thumb off the button to release the line NOW!

5 After each cast, retrieve your sinker by cranking the handle on the reel in a clockwise direction. Depending on which hand you cast with and which side the reel handle is on, you may have to switch hands after casting to put the rod and reel in the hand that is most comfortable for holding it while the other hand does the cranking.

1 foot

sinker detail

6 Keep turning the handle to rewind the line until the sinker is dangling a foot or so from the rod tip. Now you're ready for another cast.

PRACTICE MAKES PERFECT

Once you have the motion and the timing of the release figured out, start trying to make longer casts. Practice accuracy, keeping track of how many casts you make before you hit a target. Here are some tips.

If the sinker sails too high into the air, you are taking your thumb off the button too soon.

Use a plastic hoop (or a circle of rope, or a trash can lid) as a target.

If the sinker hits the ground right in front of you, you are holding on to the button too long.

Some casting plugs look like fish!

CASTING OR CATCHING?

Some people who like to cast don't even go fishing! Casting, all on its own, is a sport among groups who form casting clubs and hold contests and exhibitions across the nation. You can learn more from the American Casting Association website.

TIME TO Go Fishing!

Now that you've gathered your fishing tackle, practiced casting with your rod, and you know where to buy or find your own bait, it's time to get out and catch some fish!

In this chapter you'll learn how to bait your hook, fix the bobber, and land a fish.

Start on Shore

Good fishing can be found in ponds, streams, lakes, reservoirs, canals, and rivers. No matter where you decide to try your luck, let's begin by fishing from the shore or bank. The panfish we are targeting live in shallow water along the shoreline where they can find cover, or "structure," such as rocks, stumps, brush, boat docks, fallen trees, and water plants or weeds. Structure offers both baitfish and gamefish hiding places, shade from the sun, and food in the form of aquatic insects and tiny fish that live there.

Some of the best fishing can be found on docks or fishing platforms built along the shore. They offer man-made structure, such as concrete or wood posts, that attracts fish. Many docks allow you to access deeper water than you might be able to reach from the shore, and they often have places to sit or to store your rods, poles, and tackle while fishing.

CHECK THE REGULATIONS

It's important to check your local fishing regulations to make sure you are following the rules. Most states allow people up to around age 16 to fish without a license. Some offer free fishing days, usually in the spring or early summer, when people of any age may fish without a license. Also, some states don't allow you to keep some species of gamefish you might catch during certain weeks or months, called closed seasons. Check with your local fish and wildlife agency to see what regulations are in place in your area and for tips on where to fish.

Scout Out a Good Spot

As you search along the shore for a place to set up for fishing, look for areas with easy access to the water and no trees close overhead. Unless you are careful, branches will catch and tangle your line as you try to cast or swing it out into the water, which can be very frustrating! You also want to be able to cast your bait to a spot close to weeds, rocks, stumps, or other structure in the water.

I recommend starting at a local lake or pond for your first fishing trips. Streams and rivers are good places to catch fish, but the moving water makes it harder to keep your bait where you want it and can cause you to snag your hook on things that the water pushes your bait into. If you do choose a river for your first fishing trips, try to select an area where there is deep water and little current.

See the maps on the next pages to get an idea of where fish might be found in a lake or stream.

A great resource for finding good places to fish is the local office of your state's fish and wildlife agency. Many state and community parks have ponds that are managed for fishing, too. Some even offer special children's fishing areas and docks that are perfect for learning how to catch fish.

RIVER RULES

Be extra careful when fishing in rivers and streams. A strong current can sometimes sweep your feet out from under you, causing you to fall. Underwater rocks can be slippery, causing you to turn an ankle.

The depth of flowing water can change quickly, going from shallow to deep in one step. And if you lose your footing and fall into the water, a strong current can actually carry you away.

You may be tempted to wade out into the water to cool off on a hot day or to reach a certain spot where you'd like to fish, but that can be dangerous. If you do try wading, make sure you are wearing a life vest, or personal flotation device (PFD), and be careful where you walk.

WHERE ARE THE FISH IN A LAKE?

- **Fish want to hang out** in places where there is food to eat, protection from the elements, and the temperature is comfortable. If you find a spot that offers all three, you will find fish. Catching them is up to you!

- **Fish mostly feed** on minnows, insects, worms, crayfish, snakes, tadpoles, frogs, and even smaller versions of each other, known as "fry." Larger freshwater fish will eat mice, voles, and small birds that fall into the water. Since most of these food items can be found along the shore, that is a great place to start fishing.

- **Fish need protection** from predators and the bright sun. Predators include larger fish that may eat them, fish-eating mammals such as otters and mink, amphibians such as alligators and turtles, and us! That's why fish often are found in the branches of fallen trees or weeds, around submerged stumps or boulders, or in the shade of boat docks.

- **Fish like streams.** A good place to try to find fish in a lake or pond is where small streams, called tributaries, flow into it. Stream water is cooler than the lake most of the year but may be warmer in the spring and fall, and then fish will seek it to be comfortable. Tributary streams also carry food like worms, minnows, and insects into the lake water, and fish know to hang out nearby.

- **Fish seek out cooler water in summer.** Some species, such as crappies, white bass, and walleyes, move to deeper, cooler, darker waters in hot weather. They can often be found hunting near schools of shad or minnows.

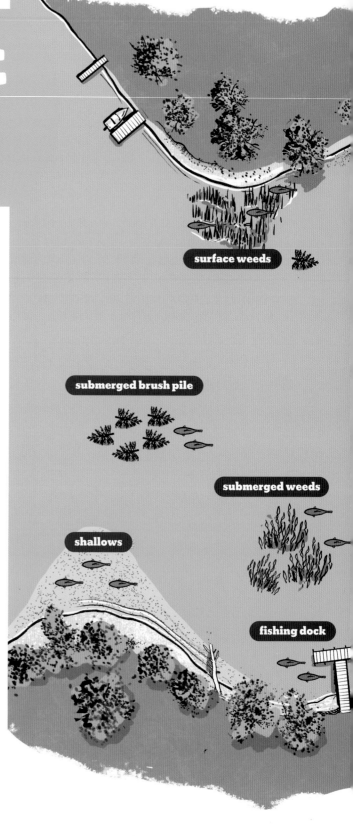

surface weeds

submerged brush pile

submerged weeds

shallows

fishing dock

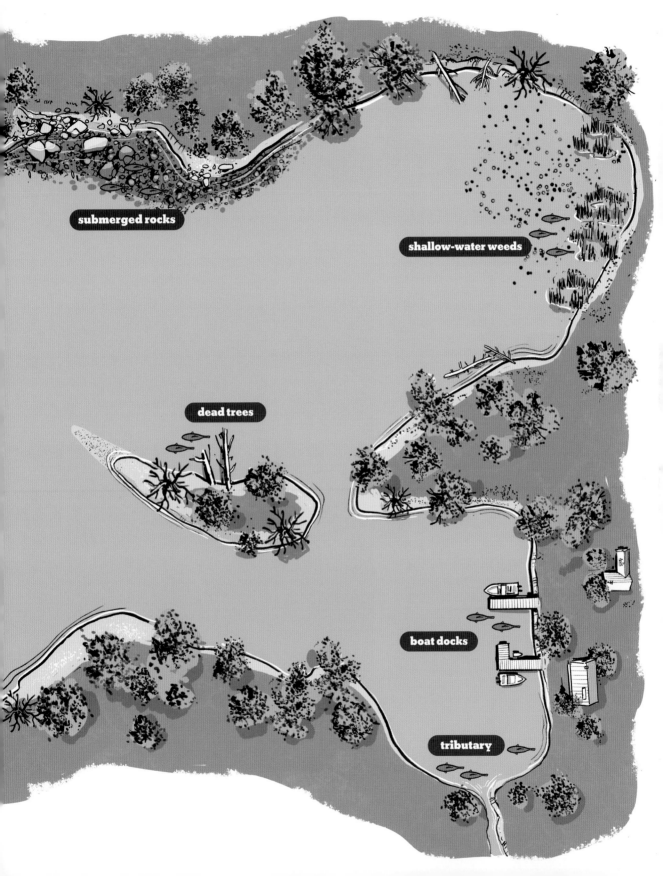

WHERE ARE THE FISH IN A STREAM?

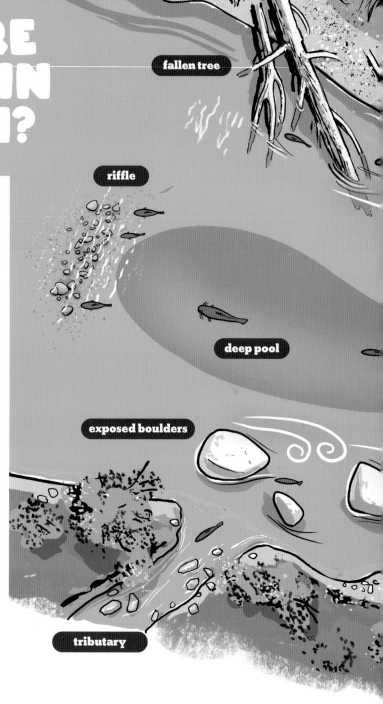

fallen tree

riffle

deep pool

exposed boulders

tributary

- **Playing hide-and-seek.** Fish are often found hiding in streams and rivers among the branches of fallen trees or weeds, around submerged stumps or boulders, or in the shade of boat docks. That's where they find protection from predators and the bright rays of the sun.

- **Resting in the riffles.** Look for fish in the pools of deeper, slower-moving water that is usually downstream of areas known as riffles. Riffles are shallow areas where the water moves over rocks and gravel often faster than it moves in the pool. This water motion washes bait-fish, insect larvae, worms, and other food from the rocks and into the pool down-stream. The movement of the water over the shallows also helps add oxygen to the water, which fish like.

- **Waiting for dinner.** Some stream fish species, such as smallmouth bass, trout, and sunfish, will hide downstream behind boulders and logs that are either completely sunken on the bottom or are only partly covered by water. The fish stay in the calm water downstream of this cover and wait for food to float by.

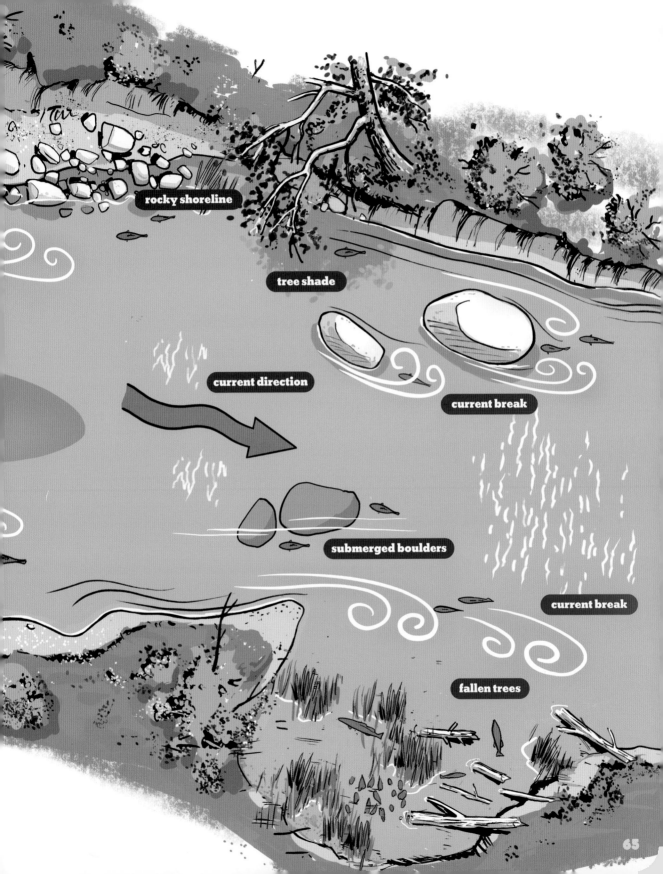

rocky shoreline

tree shade

current direction

current break

submerged boulders

current break

fallen trees

HOLIDAY STRUCTURE

Trees that fall into the water make excellent structure for fish to hide and feed around. For this reason, many communities and state fishery agencies collect Christmas trees each winter, attach them to cement blocks so they will sink, and set them out in waterways.

In northern states where most waterways are frozen in winter, the trees are placed on the ice over the areas that need more underwater structure. When the ice melts in the spring, the trees sink down to the bottom.

Set Up for Success

Fishing rods and poles are fragile, especially their tips, which can break if stepped on or poked against things like trees or docks. Always carry your fishing rod with its tip pointed up so it won't accidentally hit something (or someone!).

When you arrive at your fishing spot, organize your tackle so that everything you need is handy and in a safe place.

• Place your **bait container** in a shady spot where it will remain cool.

• Put your **tackle box** nearby but not so close that you may trip on it while casting or landing a fish.

• If you are using a **landing net**, place it near the water and within reach of where you'll be standing.

• If you want to keep some fish for eating later, set up your **bucket** or **stringer** near the shore. (See page 90 to learn about keeping your catch alive.)

• Keep your **needle-nose pliers** in a pocket, on your belt in a pliers holster, or nearby for easy access.

• Tuck a **towel** in your back pocket where you can reach it easily to dry or clean your hands.

towel

tackle box

net

needle-nose pliers

bait box

stringer

HOW TO Bait a Hook

How you put bait on your hook depends on what kind of bait you're using. Here we'll review the different techniques to get bait properly on the hook so that it stays put when you cast it into the water.

HOOKING A WORM

1. Hold the fat end of the worm between your thumb and index finger in one hand. It will squirm around a little bit, so you'll have to pinch it lightly to hold it.

2. Hold the hook between the thumb and index finger of your other hand. Carefully put the point of the hook on the worm, between the thumb and finger that are holding the worm. Push the point of the hook through the worm and out the other side.

3. If the worm is long enough, hook it again at a point farther down its body.

HOOKING MEALWORMS OR GRUBS

1 Hook a mealworm just like a regular worm; see the facing page. You can put on two or three at a time.

2 Another method is to push the hook into one end of the mealworm and slide the mealworm over the hook until the point just starts to come out the other end.

Mealworms and grubs are small, so use a small hook when using them for bait. A size 10 or 12 is about right.

How to Bait a Hook continued

continued

HOOKING A MINNOW

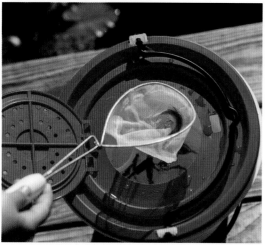

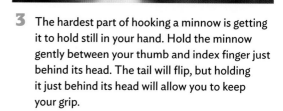

1 Start with a bait bucket of minnows and a dip net, which is a small net with a short wire handle.

2 Take a minnow out of your minnow bucket. You can net one minnow at a time or pull out a bunch of them and select which minnow you want to use for bait.

3 The hardest part of hooking a minnow is getting it to hold still in your hand. Hold the minnow gently between your thumb and index finger just behind its head. The tail will flip, but holding it just behind its head will allow you to keep your grip.

4 Method 1: To keep the minnow alive and wiggling while it's on the hook, put the point through its lips, up from the bottom lip or chin and out through its nose. Don't put the hook too far back toward the head.

Method 2: You can also hook a minnow through the skin on its back just under the top, or dorsal, fin. Don't put the hook too deep into its body or it won't wiggle enough and may die on the hook.

HOW TO Set a Bobber

Begin by setting your bobber to suspend the bait about 2 feet under the surface of the water. That is a good depth for finding hungry panfish, and it's an easy length of line to handle when casting.

ROUND BOBBER

1   The bobber has a tiny, spring-loaded wire clip on each end. Push the button on the top of the bobber to expose the clip on the bottom.

After baiting the hook, attach a bobber to your line.

bottom clip

button

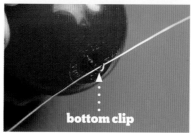

bottom clip

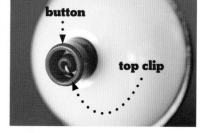

button

top clip

Some anglers attach the bobber with both clips, but for kids, using just the lower clip is a great way to start.

2   Slip the clip over the line and release the button to hold the bobber in place on the line. Start with the bobber 2 feet above the hook.

If you want to fish deeper, move the bobber farther away from the hook. To fish shallower, move the bobber closer to the hook. You may need to pinch the button to allow the line to slide easily through the bobber's clip.

bobber

2 feet

baited hook

How to Set a Bobber continued

STICK BOBBER

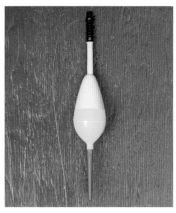  

1   To attach a spring-type stick bobber, shown here, push down the coiled spring to expose the slot in the bottom of the bobber's stick, and place your line into the slot.

2   Release the spring. It will hold the line tight in the bobber. You can usually slide a stick bobber up and down your line without removing it, but you may need to push the spring down to release its grip on the line.

stick bobber

WHEN DO YOU USE A STICK BOBBER?

Anglers who want to place their bait very close to the bottom use stick bobbers because the way they float tells you if they are set the way you want them. Stick bobbers are designed to float upright, with one end under the surface and the other end pointing straight up above the water.

If your bait is resting on the bottom, the stick bobber will sit at an angle or even float flat on top of the water, since the weight of the terminal tackle (the bait, hook, and any sinkers) is supported by the bottom instead of the bobber.

You can fine-tune experimenting with the bobber's placement on the line. You want to find the spot that allows the bobber to float upright while holding the bait just above the bottom, where fish will be attracted to it. You may need to add a split shot or two to your line to give it enough weight to float the stick bobber in the proper upright position, yet not so much weight that it pulls the bobber under.

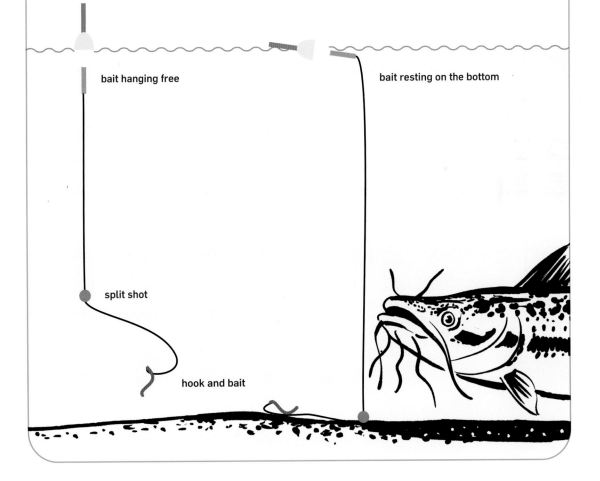

bait hanging free

bait resting on the bottom

split shot

hook and bait

COMMON BOBBER RIGS

Plan for what type of fish you want to catch.

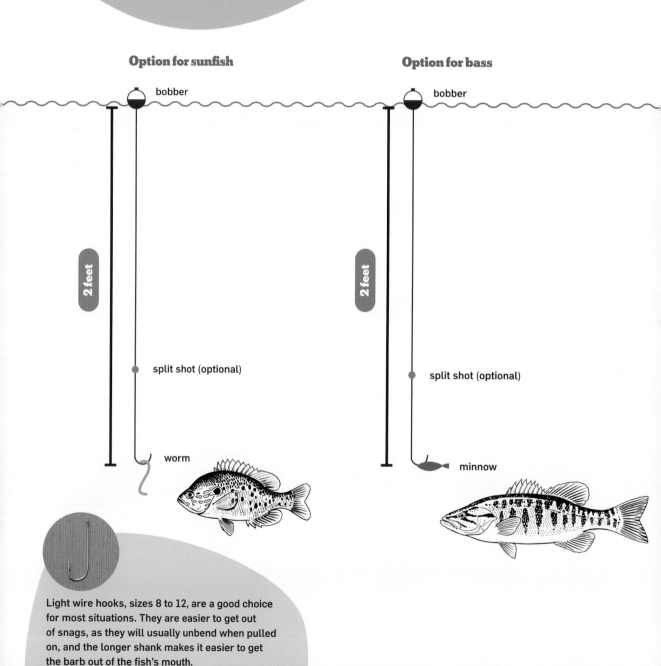

Option for sunfish

bobber

2 feet

split shot (optional)

worm

Option for bass

bobber

2 feet

split shot (optional)

minnow

Light wire hooks, sizes 8 to 12, are a good choice for most situations. They are easier to get out of snags, as they will usually unbend when pulled on, and the longer shank makes it easier to get the barb out of the fish's mouth.

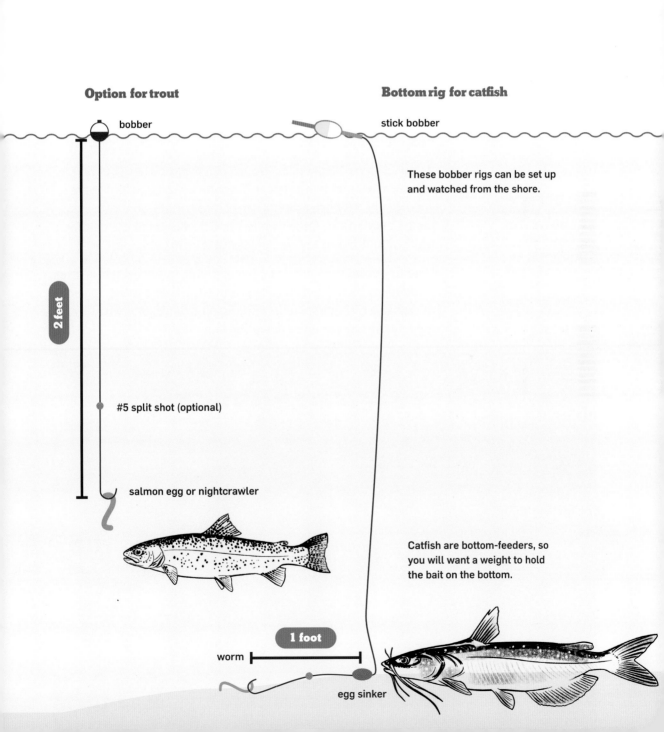

Option for trout

bobber

2 feet

#5 split shot (optional)

salmon egg or nightcrawler

worm

1 foot

Bottom rig for catfish

stick bobber

These bobber rigs can be set up
and watched from the shore.

Catfish are bottom-feeders, so
you will want a weight to hold
the bait on the bottom.

egg sinker

Cast Your Line

Once all your tackle is in place, it's time to fish! If you've practiced casting at home (see Chapter 3), you should be able to place your bait where you want it in the water. All you have to do now is put bait on your hook and a bobber on your line and cast away!

In spring and fall, fish are usually found closer to the surface than they are during the summer. When the air is warmer and water temperatures go up, they seek out deeper, cooler water. When the sun is bright and air temperature is high, fish may move into shady water in the shallows, such as among thick weeds or far back under boat docks.

If you've chosen a good location, a fish will soon see your bait and swim over to investigate it. Sometimes, especially if there are other hungry fish around, the fish will attack and try to eat the bait right away. Other times, the fish will watch the bait for a while or nibble at it before deciding if it wants to eat it.

I like to give each cast at least five minutes to see if a fish is interested in my bait. Then I may reel it in a few feet and wait again, or cast to a different place, or change the depth of my bait by moving the bobber up or down the line.

If your first few casts don't go as far as you want, just reel in the line and try again. If you are using an artificial bait or lure, you must keep the fake bait moving so that it looks alive to fool the fish into trying to eat it.

Fishing takes patience. You have to give the fish a chance to find your bait.

bobber

The bobber may move with the current or the breeze, but you'll learn to tell the difference between those movements and a fish striking at the bait.

A REEL DRAG

All fishing reels have an adjustable drag, a kind of brake that automatically releases line under tension when a big fish strikes. The drag tension—that is, how hard a fish has to pull to release more line from the reel—is set using a dial or some other sort of mechanism on your reel. The drag allows a strong fish to pull line off the spool even while you are reeling it in, which helps keep the fish from breaking the line.

The drag is set based on the strength of the fishing line on the reel, usually at about half or a little higher than its tested breaking strength. For example, if you are using 10-pound line, you would set the drag to release line at 5 to 7 pounds of pull pressure. You can use a hand scale to set the drag, but most anglers do it by feel, setting the drag to allow them to pull line from the reel with a hard, steady pull.

drag adjustment dial

Set the Hook

Once you have fooled a fish into biting your baited hook, you must set the hook—make sure it is stuck in the fish's mouth—before trying to reel it in. To do this, reel in the line just enough to feel tension on the end. When the line is stretched straight between the rod and the fish, lift the rod quickly to jab the hook into the fish's mouth.

Be sure that the line between the rod and the fish is fairly tight before you set the hook, or the hook may not stick in the fish's mouth. Sometimes a fish will bite hard enough to hook itself, but always check that the hook is set before you begin to reel in the line.

Keep It Up

If you try to set the hook and it doesn't stick in the fish's mouth, you may lose the fish. In that case, stop lifting the rod or reeling in the line and let the bobber sit for a few moments. Often a fish will return, and if there is still bait on the hook, it will hit it again, giving you a second chance.

If your bobber and hook fly out of the water when you try to set the hook, it means you missed the fish's strike. Check your hook. If it is bare, that means a fish has eaten the bait without getting hooked, and it's time to re-bait and try again.

WATCH THE BOBBER!

When panfish such as bluegills and other sunfish attack your bait, they might pull the bobber down and out of sight. Other times the fish may swim away rather than down, pulling the bobber across the surface. In either case, a moving bobber signals that it's time to set the hook!

When the bobber sinks or moves sharply, you'll feel a tug on the line and see the pole bending.

Reel in the line just enough to feel tension on the end.

Set the hook in the fish's mouth, then start reeling in the line and see what you've caught!

Land a Fish

Once you have set the hook and have a fish on the end of your line, the fun really begins. Small panfish can be landed quickly and lifted from the water without a net, but larger species should be allowed to pull the line for a while and get tired before you try to land them.

LANDING A FISH WITH A CANE POLE

Method 1: Lift up

If the fish is small enough, you can use your pole to lift it out of the water and swing it over to land. If the fish is bigger, use your pole to lift it to the surface of the water, then scoop it out with a landing net.

Method 2: Back up

If you are fishing from shore and there is room behind you, you can slowly walk backward and slide the fish out of the water. First take a quick look behind you to make sure you won't trip over anything. Then raise your rod tip, tighten the line, and start to back up with small steps, pulling the fish onto the bank until you or your partner can grab it.

LANDING A FISH WITH A ROD AND REEL

1 Maintain a slight bend in the rod to keep the hook set in place.

2 Lift up the rod tip to pull on the line and bring the fish closer to you. Keeping a slight bend in the rod while it is overhead, start reeling in the line as you slowly lower the rod tip to keep that bend and recover the line.

3 Keep lifting and reeling until the fish is close enough to reach with a net or pull it onto shore.

LANDING IT!

Take it slow. Reeling in the fish too quickly can pull out the hook or cause the fish to wrap around something along the shore and break free. Instead, allow larger fish to get tired out in the open water before bringing them closer.

Keep it up. It's important to keep your rod tip high and the pole bent slightly at all times. The bend in the rod keeps tension on the line, and that pulling pressure helps keep the hook set in the fish's mouth.

DEALING WITH SNAGS

A snag is when you accidentally catch your hook on something in the water or, if you're casting, overhead. When you realize you have a snag, you will be tempted to start yanking on the rod to free the hook. Don't. Yanking on a snag can result in the hook flying back into your face or body, or digging deeper into what it's stuck on.

Walk upstream to free a snagged line.

The best way to try to free a snagged hook is to move, so that you're working on the hook from a different angle, and to give a strong, steady pull on the line. In a river, the current can sometimes push a baited hook under a rock or other obstacle. In this case, moving upstream and pulling the line from there will help free the snag. The steady pull will have one of two results: The hook will break free of the snag, allowing you to reel the line back in, or the line will break and you will have to re-rig.

While you're pulling on the line, look away from the snag and wear sunglasses if you have them in case it pops free and the hook, lure, or sinker comes flying back at you. You may have to tighten the drag or hold the spool so that it doesn't slip off the reel while you pull on the line.

If your line gets tangled overhead, you might be able to pull it loose rather than cutting the line and losing your hook. Always protect your eyes by turning your head away from the line as you pull.

bobber stuck in tree

Shield your eyes.

Netiquette

Netting a frisky fish can be tricky, so it's good to have a partner to help you. The best way to scoop up a fish is to submerge the hoop of the net and then drag the fish over the opening. Don't jab at the fish with the net or try to lift it out of the water before it's fully inside the net.

Be patient and let the fish get tired; it will eventually turn on its side and allow you to pull it along the surface and over the net.

When the fish is over the hoop, with the netting below it, your partner can quickly raise the net to surround the fish and lift it from the water.

HOW TO Remove the Hook

After you successfully land a fish, it's time to remove the hook. The hook will usually catch in the fish's lips or mouth, and you can often see the hook's shank. Once you're holding the fish, you can figure out the best way to remove the hook.

If you are keeping the fish, you can use a towel to hold the fish while removing the hook. Be aware that the fabric will remove the protective slime from its skin, and it may not survive if you change your mind and release it.

1 To remove the hook from a spiny panfish, dangle the fish from the line with one hand. With the thumb and index finger of your other hand, form an "OK" sign around the line above the fish.

2 Slide your circled fingers down the line to the fish's head and down its body to flatten the fins against the body while you tighten your grip to keep the fish still. Let go of the line and use that hand to take out the hook, using your fingers or needle-nose pliers.

Turn the
hook down
and unhook.

3 If you can grab the hook's shank with your thumb
and index finger, carefully back the curved part
and point out of the fish. If the hook is stuck in
the fish's throat, use the pliers to grab the shank
and gently work it out.

JUMP FOR JOY

Some gamefish jump out of the water
and into the air when they are hooked
and being reeled in. Freshwater bass
and trout and saltwater species such
as tarpon and billfish jump to try
to shake or pull the hook free. The
excitement of the jumping fish on
the line has made some of those
species very popular among catch-
and-release anglers.

In fact, some tarpon anglers remove
the hook from their lure so that when
a fish attacks it and starts jumping,
the hookless lure comes loose and the
anglers don't have to go through the
trouble of fighting and reeling in the
fish before releasing it. They fish to
experience the joy of the jump alone!

How to Remove the Hook continued

4 For a larger fish or one you plan to release, you can usually remove the hook while the fish is still in the net. That can be easier than holding the fish in your hand while unhooking it since the netting will keep the fish from moving around very much. Once the hook is removed, simply dip the net into the water deep enough to allow the fish to swim out of the hoop.

5 If you can't remove the hook without injuring the fish, use the pliers to cut the line as close to the hook as you can and let the fish free. The hook will rust or work its way out eventually, and studies have shown that fish survive much better with a hook left in their throat than they do after efforts to remove it, which can damage the gills and throat.

All fish have fins on the top, sides, and bottom of their bodies. Some panfish, such as sunfish and crappies, have stiff, sharp spines that will puncture your skin if you are not careful when handling them.

To hold a fish while you remove the hook, smooth the spines from the head down toward the tail.

If you are keeping your fish in a basket in the water or in a bucket of water on shore, put them in the container as soon as you remove the hook.

SLIME TIME

Fish have a layer of slime on their scales or skin that protects them from cuts, rashes, and infections. Wiping it off can be harmful to the fish, so you don't want to wrap a towel around a fish that you are going to release back into the water. Wetting your hands before handling a fish you want to release helps protect the slime layer.

Keeping Your Catch Alive

If you want to keep the fish you catch to eat later, it's important to keep the fish alive for as long as possible in some water (or to put them on ice right away) so that the meat stays fresh and tastes good. There are several ways to do this.

No matter what kind of stringer or basket you use to keep your catch while you continue to fish, remember to attach it to something on land so that it doesn't come loose and sink.

A basket in the water. Collapsible mesh fish baskets are popular among anglers for keeping their catch alive. Made of thin metal wire links woven into a container about the size of a pillowcase, a fish basket has a spring-loaded lid that allows you to drop fish through and keep them inside. You keep the basket in the water next to the boat or bank, and the fish can swim around while you continue fishing.

A bucket filled with water. You can use a large bucket of water to keep fish alive for short periods of time. It's fun to watch your fish swim, but you will need to add water on a regular basis to keep them alive.

A fish can "hold its breath" out of water for about the same amount of time you can hold your breath. If you're having trouble unhooking a fish, put it back in the water for a minute or two so it can get some oxygen, then keep trying.

A plastic laundry basket set in the water can also hold fish for a while.

The more fish in the bucket and the warmer the weather, the more often you have to replace the water in the bucket with fresh water from the lake or stream. That's because the water contains the oxygen that fish need to breathe, and the more fish that have to share it, or the warmer the water gets, the less oxygen it contains.

rope stringer

Stringer. A stringer allows fish to keep breathing underwater while preventing them from swimming away. The simplest type of stringer is a six-foot length of nylon or cotton cord with a metal point, or needle, at one end and a metal ring at the other. When you catch a fish, push the needle through the fish's lower jaw and out the mouth and then through the metal ring to loop it in place.

You can stack additional fish on top of the first by stringing them in the same way and sliding them down the rope to the first fish. After you've strung a fish on the line, tie the line to something on the shore and put the fish back into the water so they can breathe.

HOW TO USE A STRINGER

The lower jaw of most fish has thin skin that is easy to penetrate with the stringer's point.

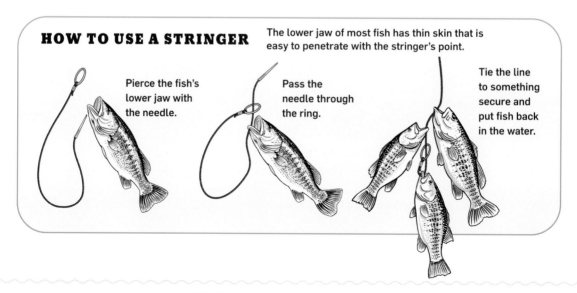

Pierce the fish's lower jaw with the needle.

Pass the needle through the ring.

Tie the line to something secure and put fish back in the water.

snap stringer

A snap stringer. This type of stringer often does a better job of keeping fish alive. It is made of thin chain or nylon cord with large metal or plastic snaps placed at intervals. The snaps are larger versions of the ones used to attach lures and hooks to fishing line. Each fish goes on a separate snap.

A **snap stringer** attaches through the lower jaw.

- Pinch open the snap to expose the sharp tip of the loop.

- Push the tip through the fish's mouth and out the jaw.

- Line up the tip with the clasp and squeeze it closed like a giant safety pin.

Now the fish is secured to your stringer, and you can drop it into the water.

Clean Your Catch

Most of the fish we catch are good to eat. There are two popular ways to clean the fish to get it ready for cooking: gutting and filleting.

GUTTING A FISH

1 With the help of an adult, use a small sharp knife to cut the fish's stomach. Start your cut at the fish's vent (the hole where it poops), and cut to where the gills come together, just behind its head.

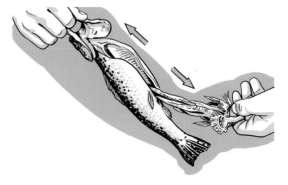

2 Holding the head with one hand, reach into the body cavity with a spoon or your fingers to pull out the internal organs, or guts.

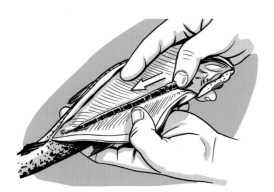

3 Run your thumb along the spine to clear away any remaining blood or guts. Once the body cavity is cleaned out, rinse the fish inside and out.

4 Use a fish scaler or a butter knife to scrape the scales off the skin.

Another way to prepare a fish is to fillet it by cutting the flesh from the body. Filleting a fish takes practice and a sharp fillet knife, which has a thin, flexible blade. When you fillet a fish, you don't have to gut it, since the meat will be cut away from each side of the fish and the bones and guts discarded together.

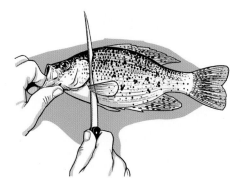

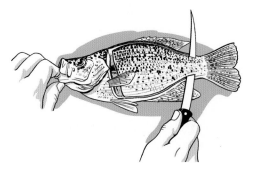

1 Place the fish on its side on a cutting board. I sometimes spread salt on the board to keep it from getting slippery from the slime coating the fish's skin. Then make the first cut, a diagonal one from just behind the gill through to the spine.

2 Turn the knife so that the sharp edge points toward the tail. Saw the knife carefully back and forth to cut the meat and skin away from the bones, taking off as much edible flesh as possible. Slice all the way to the tail, creating a fillet (strip) of meat and skin. Flip the fish over and repeat the process on the other side. If the rib cage is attached after you cut the fillet, remove it with the knife, before or after removing the skin. Discard the carcass.

3 To remove the skin, lay the fillet flat on the cutting board skin-side down. Working from either end of the fillet, insert the knife's cutting edge between the skin and the meat and work it toward the opposite end.

Keep the blunt back edge of the knife pushed down on the skin and the sharp end tilted up just enough to cut through the meat above and leave the skin below. If you do it right, you will be left with a skinless, boneless fillet of fish that can be prepared in lots of different ways.

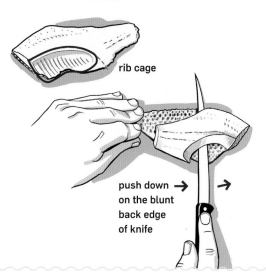

rib cage

push down → →
on the blunt
back edge
of knife

How to Cook Your Catch

Here are a few easy and popular methods to cook fish. If you want to learn more about preparing and cooking fish, check your local library for books or look for resources online.

KITCHEN COOKING

A common way to cook a whole panfish is to dip the cleaned fish in milk, then in flour or cornmeal, or in a batter made of milk and flour, and place it in a frying pan holding ¼ inch of hot oil. (Note: Having the fish and the batter cold helps the coating stick better.)

Once the bottom side is cooked and the skin crispy, carefully flip the fish over and cook the other side. Remove the fish, place it on a paper towel to soak up any extra oil, and it's ready to serve! The skin will peel off and the white meat will be flaky and easy to remove with a fork.

You can also drop skinless fillets coated in batter into a deep fryer or an air fryer. Baking fish in the oven with vegetables is another great way to enjoy your catch.

CAMPFIRE COOKING

Heat a cast-iron pan over a grill set on a campfire. Add a few large pats of butter and place the whole fish right into the pan. If you'd like, you can also add a chopped garlic clove and a drizzle of olive oil. The fats will keep the fish from sticking to the pan and make the skin a little crispy.

Cook the fish for 3 to 4 minutes per side and then take it out of the pan. Top with salt and pepper and a squeeze of lemon and enjoy your fresh catch!

HOW TO
Think like a Fish

How much do you know about fish? A good angler learns about what kinds of fish live nearby, what they like to eat, and where to find them. In this chapter, you'll find details about some common fish that can be found in many parts of North America.

The freshwater fish you are most likely to catch include sunfish, crappies, bass, catfish, and trout. Most beginning anglers get started with sunfish, which include bluegills, green sunfish, and redears.

AVOIDING LIGHT

Most fish don't have eyelids to open and close and thus control the amount of light that reaches their eyes. This is one reason why, when sunlight is strong, fish look for shade. They might go under a dock, find the shady side of a rock or stump, or swim to a deeper spot where the sunlight can't penetrate the water.

Knowing where fish find shade can tell you where to drop your bait the next time you go fishing on a sunny day.

Comfort Zones

Unlike humans, who are warm-blooded, fish are cold-blooded, which means their bodies can adjust to the temperature of the water they live in. However, fish of different species still have a temperature range they prefer. If the water around them gets too warm or too cold, most fish move more slowly and don't eat as much, so they can be harder to catch.

Just like us, fish like to be comfortable. They seek out places where the water temperature suits them and the light is not too bright. They also like to be near the food they eat, whether that is a place where minnows hang out, a spot where rains can wash worms and insects into the water from the shore, or an area where the current brings baitfish, crayfish, or insects to them.

Fish may move throughout the day to locate such areas, which is why sometimes you will get lots of bites in the morning in one spot, but no action there at a different time of the day. That's part of the fun of fishing: figuring out where the fish are, when, and why.

It's Fishing Season!

Where most people go fishing in North America, water temperatures are warmest in the summer and coldest in the winter. That is why some of the best fishing takes place in the spring and in the fall, when water temperatures aren't too hot or too cold.

The spring and early summer are especially good times to fish for most species. That's because most fish start feeding again after the winter months as the sun warms the waters around them. Most fish species also spawn, or lay their eggs, in the spring, so they need to eat more to keep up their strength and produce healthy offspring.

Fish feed more in the fall, too, because with colder weather coming, they need to put on weight to help get through winter. Colder water makes it harder for them to find smaller baitfish, worms, insects, and other sources of food.

Off-Season Fishing

That doesn't mean that midsummer and winter aren't good times to go fishing. It's just that both fish and anglers are more comfortable when air and water temperatures aren't too hot or too cold.

In the summer, when the strong sun warms up the water at the surface, most fish move to deeper water, where the temperature is more comfortable for them. To catch these fish, you must place your bait deeper. If you've had several unsuccessful casts, try moving the bobber up your line, six inches at a time, until you find the depth where the fish are hanging out—and hopefully waiting to eat what you have on your hook!

In the winter, the opposite can be true: Fish may seek out warmer water, which can be in the shallows where the sun heats it. In areas where it is cold enough for lakes and rivers to freeze over, people go ice fishing.

Ice Fishing

ICE FISHING is a fun way to keep fishing all year in the same lakes and ponds where you caught fish during the regular fishing season. Ice anglers fish through round holes cut through the ice using a big drill called an auger.

Ice anglers use short fishing rods and bring their catch in by pulling the line up hand over hand. Some also use ice fishing devices called tip-ups that are placed over the holes and drop a line to the depth set by the angler. When a fish takes the bait under a tip-up, a small flag tips or springs up to alert the angler that a fish has been hooked below the ice.

To keep warm on the frozen water, many ice anglers set up shanties, small structures with room for one or more anglers to sit and fish. The shanties are placed over the ice holes and may have portable heaters inside. More elaborate ice fishing shanties have televisions, bunks, and cooking facilities so that the anglers can stay out on the ice for days at a time!

Ice fishing is fun, but also risky. If the ice isn't thick enough, you can break through into dangerously cold water with no easy way to get out. Wear a PFD, never ice fish alone, and only go with anglers who are experienced at ice fishing and have the proper tackle and safety equipment.

FISH YOU MIGHT CATCH

Most fish, such as sunfish, trout, and crappies, swim near the surface in the morning and the evening in summer. During the middle of the day, they move deeper in the water.

Largemouth and smallmouth bass can be found at various depths depending on where they want to feed or rest.

Smallmouth Bass

Largemouth Bass

Catfish like to stay and feed near the bottom of the lake or river pretty much all the time and are most active at night.

Catfish

Crappie

Sunfish

Pumpkinseed

Rainbow Trout

Trout are most active
early and late in the day.

Striped Bass

SUNFISH

Sunfish are a group of small, colorful fish that includes bluegills, redears, warmouths, pumpkinseeds, and others. They are found across much of North America and rarely weigh more than 1 pound. Sunfish will eat just about any live bait they find and put up a good fight for fish their size. They also taste good!

Where to find them: Sunfish can be found near shore year-round, making them great targets for bank anglers.

Best bait: Popular bait for sunfish includes earthworms, pieces of nightcrawlers, grubs such as mealworms, small minnows, crickets, and pieces of hot dog.

CRAPPIE

Crappies (pronounced "croppies") grow larger than sunfish, often weighing a pound or more, and taste great.

Where to find them: Crappies can be caught near the shore, but mostly in the spring when they come into the shallow waters to spawn around brush and fallen trees. When they are done spawning and the water begins to warm, they move to deeper water and form large schools. That's when you may need a boat to get to them!

Best bait: Crappies prefer small minnows and grubs or small jigs and lures that imitate baitfish.

Largemouth Bass

BASS

Bass are the most popular freshwater gamefish in the world. There are three main types that you might hook: largemouth bass, smallmouth bass, and striped bass. Bass can be big; 10-pound largemouths are not uncommon, though smallmouth and striped bass don't grow quite that large.

Although bass taste fine, most anglers practice catch and release with bass, enjoying the fight but freeing the fish so that it can grow and provide more fun fishing in the future.

Where to find them: Bass can be found around shoreline cover year-round. They like to hang out among weed beds, fallen trees, boat docks, and other structures that offer shade and a place to hide and wait for food to swim past or fall into the water.

Smallmouth Bass

Striped Bass

Smallmouth and striped bass are more likely to be found in rivers and other moving water. They prefer cooler water than do largemouth bass. That's why you mostly find smallmouth bass in the cooler northern parts of the country, and largemouths in the warmer areas.

Best bait: Large minnows or a whole nightcrawler make great bait for largemouth and striped bass, as do live frogs. They also will strike many kinds of artificial lures. Largemouth bass fight very hard when hooked and jump to try to shake the hook loose, which makes for an exciting catch!

Smallmouth bass like to eat crayfish and minnows and are famous for their ferocious attacks on artificial bait. Some anglers claim that smallmouth bass are the hardest-fighting freshwater fish, jumping, running, and shaking their heads to get rid of a hook.

Bullhead

CATFISH

There are many types of catfish, including blue, bullhead, channel, and flathead. Catfish got their name from their long whiskers, like those you'd see on a cat. While most gamefish have scales, catfish have smooth skin that's covered with taste buds, which, along with their sensitive whiskers, help them find food as they swim along the bottom.

Blue and flathead catfish can grow to more than 100 pounds. Channel cats, the most popular among anglers, can grow to be up to 50 pounds, though most weigh less than 10 pounds. Bullheads rarely weigh more than a pound or two. Catfish are hard fighters, and people love to eat them!

Where to find them: Catfish live at the bottom of lakes and slow-moving rivers. The best times to fish for them are early and late in the day and at night, because their eyes are very sensitive to sunlight and they use their sense of smell, instead of sight, to find their food.

Best bait: Nightcrawlers, minnows, and prepared bait work well for catching bullheads and channel catfish, while larger live baits, such as chubs or sunfish, or chunks of fresh fish are used to catch blues and flatheads. Anglers also use commercial and homemade stink bait (very strong-smelling prepared bait) and raw chicken liver to tempt catfish.

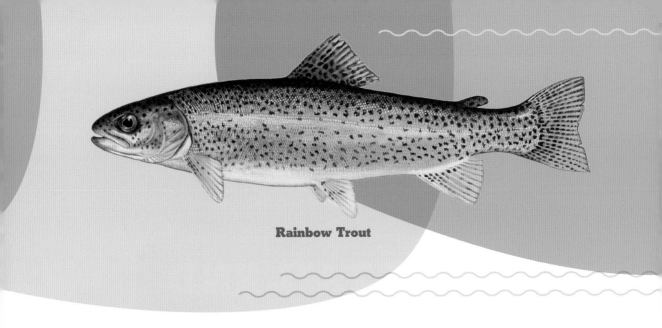

Rainbow Trout

TROUT

Trout are a prized catch anywhere you find them, and many communities stock trout in local waters each year to offer anglers the chance to catch them. Trout live in cooler water, which is why you primarily find them in lakes and streams in northern regions or at higher elevations.

The more popular species include brook trout, rainbow trout, brown trout, and lake trout. Most weigh less than 5 pounds or so and a 10-pound trout is a trophy! Lake trout can grow to 50 pounds, though these giants are usually found only in the open water of deep, cool northern lakes.

Where to find them: Rainbow and brown trout are the most common species and are usually caught from streams, ponds, and lakes. Brook trout, which generally weigh in at less than 5 pounds, prefer the cold streams and ponds of northern regions.

Best bait: Trout can be caught using live bait, such as worms and minnows, and small artificial lures. They are very popular with fly anglers, who fool them with lures called "flies," which are made from feathers and fur tied to small hooks.

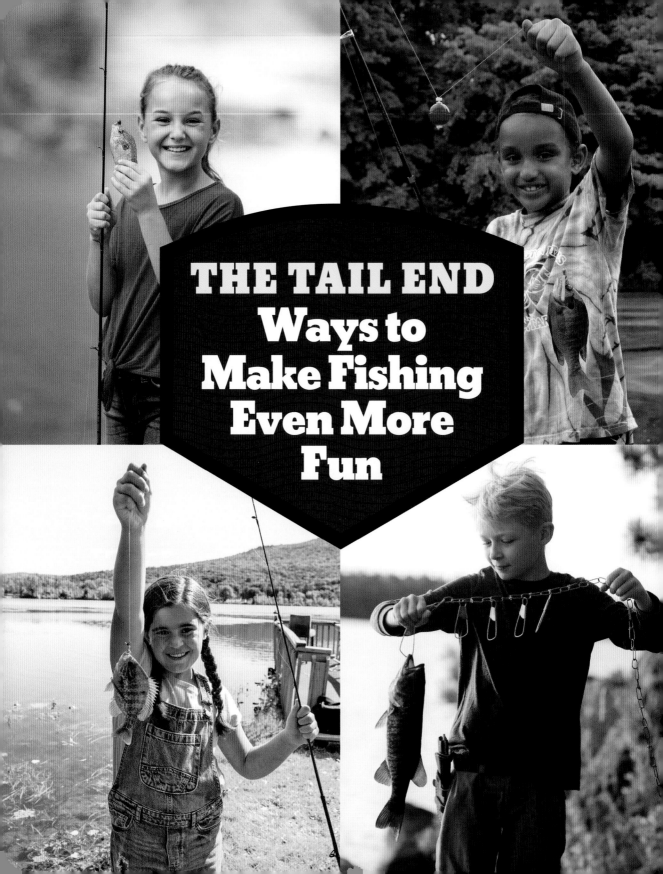

THE TAIL END
Ways to Make Fishing Even More Fun

Take Great Photos

It's fun to document your angling experience, from practicing your casting at home to gathering or buying bait, arriving at the fishing spot, and setting up for the day's fishing. Then, of course, you will want to have plenty of pictures of what you catch to help you remember the day.

A "hero shot" is a photograph of an angler proudly holding a fish. Here are some tips for taking good hero shots.

Hats off. Ask the angler to take off their hat or tip it way back, or use the flash function on the camera. Otherwise, their face will be covered by the shadow from the hat.

Set up for good light. Try to put the sun behind the camera so that it lights up the angler.

Focus! Focus the camera lens on the fish's eye to make sure that the most important part of the picture—the fish—is in sharp focus.

Keep it clean. Wipe off any dirt, grass, or blood from the fish to make a more appealing picture, and hold it so the side, not the belly, is facing the camera.

Keep it level. If there is water in the background, make sure it is level in the viewfinder.

Hold it up. For a large fish, have the angler hold the fish gently, using both hands to support it from underneath in a natural swimming position.

An Angler's Glossary

Angler. A person who fishes.

Artificial bait. *See* Lure

Bail. The part of a spinning reel that guides the line off of and back onto the spool.

Baitfish. Small fish that game-fish eat. Examples are minnows and chubs.

Barb. A small raised point along the bend of a hook, and sometimes on its shank, to keep the bait in place or help the hook stay in a fish's mouth.

Bobber. A float that you clip on to a fishing line to keep the bait at a certain depth and to show you, by its motion, when a fish has taken the bait.

Cane pole. A long pole fitted with a line of equal length and a hook.

cast

Cast. To toss a baited line out into the water.

Casting plug. A hookless weight that is attached to a line for casting practice.

Catch and release. The practice of returning the fish you catch to the water instead of keeping them to eat.

Chub. A popular baitfish that is found mostly in streams and rivers.

Combo. A combination of a rod and reel or a jig and bait. Examples are a spincast rod and reel combo or a jig and minnow combo.

Crayfish. A kind of tiny crusta-cean. Also known as crawdads, they look like small lobsters, and fish love them.

Drag. A device on a fishing reel that allows a fish to pull line from the reel under a certain amount of tension. It is designed to keep the line from breaking when a large fish is hooked.

Ferrule. A metal connector on fishing poles and rods that allows them to be taken apart for storage or transport and reconnected when it's time to fish.

Fillet. A slice of meat cut from the side of a fish.

Fry. Baby (less than 1 year old) fish of all species.

Gamefish. Fish species that anglers like to catch because they fight hard or taste good—or both! Examples are bass, trout, panfish, and catfish.

Handline. A fishing line held in the hand, without a rod or reel.

Jig. A hook with a weight attached to it, and often with a tail made of fur, feather, or plastic attached to the shank.

Landing net. A tool with a handle, hoop, and netting for lifting fish from the water.

Larva. An insect in the stage after it hatches but before it changes into its adult form. Mealworms and other grubs are examples of larvae.

Line. Also called fishing line. A string-like material that comes in various test strengths for catching different types of fish.

Line guides. Small wire hoops, attached at intervals along a fishing rod, that guide the line along the length of the rod to keep it from tangling and to make casting easier.

Line test. The amount of weight that it takes to break fishing line. For example, a 10-pound test line will break when 10 pounds of weight or tension is placed on it.

Live bait. Bait that is alive when it is put on the hook. Examples are worms, minnows, crickets, crayfish, and frogs.

Lure. An artificial bait that is designed to look like something a fish would eat. Lures can be made of metal, plastic, rubber, fur, feathers, and other materials. Examples are rubber worms, jigs, and flies.

cane pole

handlining

Panfish. Any fish, such as sunfish or crappies, that is small enough to fit in a frying pan.

Prepared bait. An artificial dough-like substance with scent and color that attract fish. Commercial brands, such as PowerBait, can be formed into balls.

Recreational fishing. Fishing for fun rather than for food.

Reel. The device near the butt end of the fishing rod that holds the fishing line, allowing it to be released or rewound.

Reel seat. The part of the rod where the reel is fastened.

Riffle. An area of shallow, disturbed water where a river or stream flows over rocks or gravel.

Rig. To attach the line to a rod or pole and add the hook, bobber, and other terminal tackle before fishing.

Rod butt. The thick end of the fishing rod, where the angler holds it.

Scaler. A handheld device that is used to remove scales from a fish's skin.

School. A gathering of fish, usually of the same species.

Sinker. A weight that is placed on a line to help the bait sink to a certain level or stay in place on the bottom.

Snag. When your hook gets caught on an object, like a clump of weeds or a tree branch, underwater or in the air, and becomes stuck.

Spool. The part of the reel that holds the wound-up line.

Stink bait. Prepared bait that has a strong smell to attract bottom-feeding gamefish such as catfish.

Stock. To place live fish, such as trout or catfish, in lakes or rivers to help populate them with gamefish.

Stringer. A line to which fish can be attached and kept alive in the water while the angler continues to fish.

Structure. Underwater objects that attract and protect fish. Examples include stumps, boulders, dock posts, and sunken trees.

Tackle. The tools that anglers use to help them catch fish, such as rods, reels, needle-nosed pliers, and stringers.

Tadpole. A larva of a frog that lives in and breathes water, also known as a polliwog.

Terminal tackle. Accessories that are placed on or near the end of the fishing line. Examples are hooks, sinkers, and bobbers.

Tributary. A river or stream that enters a larger body of water.

Troll. To fish by dragging bait behind a moving boat.

Worm bedding. Dirt, shredded newspaper, moss, or commercial bedding material that is placed in a container for worms to burrow into.

live bait

panfish

BOAT SAFETY

You don't need a boat to go fishing, but here are some tips if you go offshore.

Boats offer some advantages for anglers, such as giving you access to fishing spots that aren't within casting distance of the shore. Boats also allow anglers to "troll," or tow bait behind a slow-moving boat to catch fish that may be feeding in open water.

You can fish from just about any boat, from paddlecraft like canoes and kayaks to large powerboats designed for cruising. The most important thing to keep in mind when fishing from any boat is safety. Here's what you need to know.

WEAR A LIFE JACKET

Most states require anglers under a certain age to wear a life jacket, also known as a personal flotation device (PFD), whenever they are aboard a moving boat. A properly fitted PFD will keep you afloat and face up if you accidentally fall into the water.

LISTEN TO THE CAPTAIN

It is common courtesy to ask permission from the captain or owner of a boat before coming aboard. The captain will tell you where to sit and how to stow your gear so that the weight of the passengers and equipment is evenly distributed.

KEEP YOUR SEAT

When the boat is under way, stay in your assigned spot. Ask permission before standing up or moving around the boat. Use handrails and other solid objects to help you keep your balance.

SEA LEGS AND SHORE LEGS

Be prepared for some motion under your feet even when the boat is at the dock. Becoming used to that motion is known as "getting your sea legs" because it allows you to keep your balance as the boat moves or bumps through waves. Before you know it, your legs will automatically make small adjustments so you keep your balance and can concentrate on the fishing!

Don't be surprised to find that your legs are a little wobbly when you return to shore. When the shifting movements of the boat are suddenly replaced by a stable dock or shore, it may take a few minutes for your legs and mind to get used to being on solid ground. You may even experience a rocking sensation until you get your "shore legs" back.

NO SKIDDING

The floor, or deck, of a boat can be slippery. Wear shoes with nonskid rubber soles.

Ten Tips for Parents

1. Start early.
Begin fishing lessons by visiting a local tackle store with your child, allowing them to be a part of the entire process of selecting tackle and asking around for a good place to go fishing. Look at this book together before you head out.

2. Practice on terra firma.
Practice casting, knot tying, and bobber setting at home or at a local park, where errant casts can't catch in overhead tree limbs or streamside brush, and knots and bobbers can be figured out apart from the excitement of catching a fish.

3. Keep equipment simple.
A cane pole is a great first fishing rod, especially for younger anglers. Simple spincasting tackle, such as the youth models now offered by several tackle manufacturers, is a good choice as well. Give your child their own tackle box for storing hooks, bobbers, and sinkers.

4. Leave your own gear at home (at first).
By leaving your tackle at home until your child is a confident angler, you are more likely to stay involved in your child's activities—and less tempted to get caught up in your own casting in the event the fishing is good! Instead, record the day's activities with a camera, so you can capture that most momentous of events: a child's first fish.

5. Fish from shore.
Select a spot that offers an abundance of easily caught panfish, such as bluegill, crappie, or perch. Docks or piers are excellent choices because they are clear of trees and other obstacles that snag casts, and the structures provide shade and underwater cover for fish. Open shoreline areas along ponds, lakes, and slow-moving streams can be good, too. You can, of course, go out in a boat, but keep in mind that kids need elbow room—and wiggle room—when fishing. Many will feel confined when they have to stay seated aboard a boat for any length of time.

6. Use live bait; catch fish!

Nothing catches panfish more consistently than live bait, such as worms, nightcrawlers, crickets, or minnows. Successfully catching fish encourages a child's interest in the activity, so stock up on bait that slithers, crawls, or swims. Besides, live bait is also interesting for children to touch and play with, and they should be allowed to do just that when the fishing is slow or they simply want to do something else for a while.

7. Use a bobber.

A bobber dancing on the water's surface captivates children, especially when they know what's causing it! Besides enabling the child to see as well as feel strikes, the bobber also provides some casting weight and keeps the bait off the bottom, in front of fish and away from snags.

8. Be a good scout.

Be prepared: Take plenty of snacks and drinks and different kinds of bait for variety. Pack rain gear, jackets to match the weather, hats, sunglasses, insect repellent, and sunscreen. You want your child to be as comfortable as possible during (and after) the fishing session.

9. Keep the first sessions short.

When the child says it's time to go home, go! You want these first trips to be remembered as something fun, and when the fun ends for a child, it's time to end the expedition, no matter how well the fish are biting or how early in the trip it might be.

10. Talk with your child.

During the fishing trip, talk about anything, remembering that these are important times for kids, who value their time with you (whether they show it or not). Share feelings about anything under the sun. You can discuss angling topics, like catch-and-release philosophy, fishing tactics, and what makes a bobber work, or tell just-for-fun fishing tales about the elusive whoppers in your favorite lake.

Eventually, all this easy talking on fishing trips leads to you and your child being able to have longer talks about more serious topics—and that, perhaps more than the fish you catch, is the true prize of teaching your child to fish.

My Fishing Logbook

A great way to document your fishing time and help you catch more fish in the future is to keep a fishing logbook. By noting on every fishing trip the date, time, location, weather conditions, temperatures, the bait you used, what you caught, what other wildlife you saw, and who was with you, you will create a logbook with valuable information to help you plan fishing trips in the future. You might also write down your favorite memory of the fishing day and anything funny that happened along the way.

You can make your own fishing logbook using the pages that follow. Make photocopies or download the form on **storey.com/lets-learn-to-fish**. Put the pages into a three-ring binder. Along with your notes, add photos and drawings, which will make your logbook more fun to look at for years to come!

Where I Went	Date & Time	What the Weather Was	Bait I Used	What I Caught

Where I Went	Date & Time	What the Weather Was	Bait I Used	What I Caught

Where I Went	Date & Time	What the Weather Was	Bait I Used	What I Caught

Index

A

angling, angler
  defined, 9, 39, 112
artificial bait (or lure)
  jigs, 39, 105, 112
  minnows with hooks, 38
  rubber worms, 38

B

bail, 20, 112
bait, 31–41
  artificial, 32, 38–39
  hanging free, 75
  how to bait a hook, 53, 68–70
  live, 32–37
  prepared, 32, 40–41
  resting on the bottom, 75
  stink bait, 108, 113
bait and tackle store, 13, 28, 33
  bait box, 29, 67
baitcasting reel, 21
baitfish
  defined, 112
  minnows, 35
baitholder hook, 23
barbs, 22, 112
baskets for keeping fish alive,
  90–91
bass, 99, 102, 106–7
  bobber option, 76
  hook size, 22
  jumping when hooked, 87
  largemouth, 102, 106
  rock bass, 26
  smallmouth, 102, 107
  stream hideouts, 64
  striped, 103, 107
  white, 26, 62

bluegills, 80, 99, 104, 117
boat safety, 114–15
bobbers
  bobber with stopper peg, 47
  cane pole, 16
  common bobber rigs, 76–77
  explained, 24, 112
  homemade, 25
  how to set a round bobber,
    72–73
  how to set a stick bobber,
    74
  round bobber, 13, 24
  stick bobber, 13, 16, 24–25
  stuck in a tree, 84
  watching the bobber, 80–81
  when to use a stick bobber, 75,
    77
bottle handlining, 14
bottom rig for catfish, 75, 77
bucket
  for keeping fish alive, 90–91
  minnow bucket, 29, 35, 70

C

cane pole
  bobbers, 16, 45, 47
  fishing with, 16–17
  how to cast, 48
  how to rig, 44–47
  how to tie a clinch knot, 44
  landing a fish, 82
  storing the pole, 49
casting, 19
  a bottle line, 15
  a cane pole, 48
  with a jig, 39
  plug, 47, 112

  practicing with a sinker, 53
  with a spincast rod, 54–56
  as a sport, 57
  tips, 78–79
casting reel, parts of, 21
catch and release, 18, 112
  bass fishing, 106
  discussing, 118
  the importance of slime, 90
  using barbless hooks, 22, 87
catfish, 99, 102, 108
  bait, 40
  bottom rig, 75, 77
  hook size, 22
  stink bait, 113
  using a stick bobber, 75, 77
chub, 108, 112
cleaning your catch, 94–95
clinch knot, how to tie, 46
cooking your catch, 96–97
cork bobber, 25
crappies, 99, 102–3, 105
  porcupine quill bobber, 25
  removing a hook, 89
  where to fish for, 62, 105, 117
crayfish, 62, 100, 107, 112
crickets
  best bait for, 104, 118
  making a trap, 37
Cuban yo-yo, 14

D

drag, 112
  adjustable, 19–20
  how to set and adjust drag, 79
  tightening when your line is
    snagged, 84

E

earthworms, 33–34, 104

F

ferrule, 16, 44, 112
finding fish
   comfort zones, 100
   lake hideouts, 62–63
   preference for shade, 100
   scouting a good spot, 61
   start on shore, 60
   stream hideouts, 64–65
fish basket, collapsible mesh, 90
fishing license, 60
fishing line, 13, 112
   monofilament nylon, 24
   test, 112
fishing logbook, 120–23
frogs as live bait, 107, 112

G

grubs
   for bait, 36
   how to bait a hook, 69

H

handline fishing
   bottle, 15
   Cuban yo-yo, 14
hero shot (photographing fish),
   110–11
hooks
   baitholder, 23
   barbs, 22, 112
   circle hook, 23
   hook and sinker, 16

hooking a minnow for bait,
   70–71
hooking a worm for bait, 68–69
how to remove a hook from
   a fish, 86–89
J hook, 13, 23
parts of a hook, 22
sizes, 23
treble, 23

I

ice fishing, 101

J

jigs, 39, 105, 112
jumping fish, 87

L

landing a fish
   with a cane pole, 82
   landing net, 28–29, 66, 112
   with a rod and reel, 83
level-wind reel, 21
life jackets, 114–15
line, 13, 112
   guides, 19–21, 52
   monofilament nylon, 24
   test, 112
live bait
   cricket trap, 37
   grubs, 36
   hook size for, 22
   minnows, 35
   storing tip, 15
   tip, 15
   worms, 33–34
lure. *See* artificial bait

M

meal worms, 36, 104
   how to bait a hook, 69
minnow bucket, 29, 35, 70
minnows
   artificial, 38
   hook size for, 22
   hooking for bait, 70–71
   live bait, 35
   tip, 15

N

needle-nose pliers, 28–29, 67
   removing a hook, 88
net, 12, 28–29, 67
netting a fish, 83
nightcrawlers, 33–34, 77
   best bait for, 104, 107–8, 118

P

panfish
   defined, 28, 113
   grubs for bait, 36
   live bait, 118
   prepared bait, 36
   using a bobber, 70, 80
   where to fish, 60
perch, 117
photographing fish, 110–11
pole *vs.* rod, 21
   cane pole, 16–17
porcupine quill bobbers, 25
prepared bait, 113
   how to use, 41, 47
   kitchen scraps, 40
pumpkinseed, 103

R

red worms, 33–34
redears, 99
removing a hook from a fish, 86–89
rod and reel, 13, 18–21, 29
    adjusting drag, 79
    casting reel, 21
    combo, 18, 112
    landing a fish, 83
    spincast reel, 19
    spinning reel, 20
round bobber, 13, 24
    how to set, 72–73

S

scaler, 94, 113
set up for success, 66–67
setting the hook, 80–81
sinkers, 13
    bank or dipsey, 27
    casting practice, 53
    egg sinkers, 27
    split shot, 26
slime, protective, 86, 90, 95
snags, dealing with, 84
snap swivel, 27
spincast rod and reel, 12, 19
    how to cast, 54–57
    how to rig, 50–53
    how to tie on a hook, 53
spinning reel
    parts of, 20
stick bobber, 13, 16, 24–25
    how to set, 74
    when to use, 75, 77
stink bait, 108, 113

stringer, 66–67, 90
    defined, 92, 113
    how to use, 92
    snap stringer, 93
sunfish, 99, 103–4
    bobber option, 76
    hook size, 22
    removing a hook, 89
    stream hideouts, 64
sunglasses, 29

T

tackle
    box, 12, 28–29, 67
    defined, 11–13
    terminal tackle, 27, 113
tadpoles, 62, 113
tips for parents, 117–18
troll, 113–14
trout, 99
    bobber option, 77
    jumping when hooked, 87
    rainbow, 103, 109
    stream hideouts, 64

W

walleyes, 26
where to fish
    check regulations, 60
    lake hideouts, 62–63
    river rules, 61
    scouting a good spot, 61
    from shore, 60, 117
    stream hideouts, 64–65

worms, 12
    artificial, 38
    buying, 33
    collecting, 34
    earthworms, 33–34, 104
    hook size for, 22
    how to bait worms on a hook, 68
    meal worms, 36, 69, 104
    nightcrawlers, 33–34, 77, 104,
        107–8, 118
    red worms, 33–34

Learn More Outdoor Skills

with these books from Storey

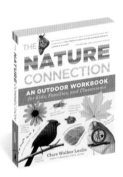

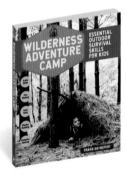

The Nature Connection
by Clare Walker Leslie

Learn to experience nature with all five senses, whether you live in the country, the city, or in between. Kids will love these engaging activities, including sketching wildlife, observing constellations, collecting leaves, keeping a weather journal, and watching bird migrations.

Sky Gazing
by Meg Thacher

This rich visual guide takes readers ages 9 to 14 on a journey through Earth's solar system, around the galaxy, and into deep space. Activities include tracking sun and moon cycles, learning to observe planets (no binoculars or telescopes required), and locating constellations in all seasons.

Wilderness Adventure Camp
by Frank Grindrod

This hands-on guidebook for kids ages 10 and up teaches essential outdoor camping and survival skills. Clear instructions and step-by-step photos demonstrate how to choose a campsite, make a fire, build a shelter, use a knife safely, cook outdoors, and much more.

Join the conversation. Share your experience with this book, learn more about Storey Publishing's authors, and read original essays and book excerpts at storey.com.

Look for our books wherever quality books are sold or call 800-441-5700.